Language and Concepts
in Christian Education

by William Bedford Williamson

The Westminster Press · *Philadelphia*

STANDARD BOOK NO. 664-20878-9

LIBRARY OF CONGRESS CATALOG CARD NO. 72-85859

PUBLISHED BY THE WESTMINSTER PRESS®
PHILADELPHIA, PENNSYLVANIA
PRINTED IN THE UNITED STATES OF AMERICA

Language and Concepts in Christian Education

In Memory of and
with Appreciation to
My Father
William Barlow Williamson
Educator and Savant
Who Prompted My Dissatisfaction
with Unexamined Attitudes and Actions

Preface

LANGUAGE AND CONCEPTS IN CHRISTIAN EDUCATION is based on my unpublished Ed.D. dissertation (Temple University, 1966) entitled "A Review of the Historical and Philosophical Foundations of the Seabury Series for Christian Education in the Protestant Episcopal Church in the United States of America." The original work is available in the library of Temple University and on microfilm, in case there are those who wish to engage in some specific scholarly disputation. The present work is an enlargement and a thoroughgoing revision, which now includes several of the major Protestant churches in its critical survey.

I write from the vantage point of a dual role. I am a clergyman, the rector of a small Episcopal parish church, and professor of philosophy at Ursinus College. I have long been interested in Christian education, as a pastor and as the chairman of a diocesan department. In my pursuit of a doctorate, I came under the influence of a leading philosophical analyst, Professor B. Paul Komisar, who introduced me to the modern role of the philosopher in education. He encouraged my dissatisfaction with all unexamined beliefs, vague and ambiguous statements, and with linguistic errors such as category shifting (an evaluation or prescription disguised as a statement of fact).

On examining the philosophical foundations of Christian education in my own church, I discovered many areas where little or no concept analysis had ever confronted the theorists. A similar examination of the comparable literature of several other churches, namely, The United Presbyterian Church in the United States of America, the Presbyterian Church in the United States, The United Methodist Church, and the Boards of Parish Education of several cooperating Lutheran Churches, revealed a glaring lack of conceptual analysis of common substantive and methodological decisions. Further, I noted a microcosmic and intramural tendency in the literature to develop artificial controversies and issues of little or no exoteric interest debated in a private language.

LANGUAGE AND CONCEPTS IN CHRISTIAN EDUCATION is intended as a challenge to open discussion on the major issues confronting the churches as they seek to fulfill their educational role. I recognize the Herculean task involved, but the difficulty of the task is no excuse for settling for emotive slogans or slogan systems. The layman should be able to read this work with profit. Indeed, perhaps like the boy in Hans Christian Andersen's tale who could not see the emperor's "magic clothes," the layman will be able to resist the sophistication of accepting nonsense disguised as explanation.

It is with sincere pleasure and gratitude that I acknowledge the helpful contributions of many persons to the accomplishment of this publication. I am grateful to the members of my sponsoring committee at Temple University: Professors B. Paul Komisar, James E. McClellan, and Arthur Blumberg, for their encouragement, counsel, and invaluable suggestions regarding the materials, the method, and the overall task development of my dissertation and, therefore, of the present volume.

I wish to thank the Reverend Mayo Y. Smith; the Reverend William J. Fischler; the Reverend Daniel B. Stevick; Professor Walter K. Malone, S.T.D., Ph.D.; Professor George G. Storey, Ph.D.; Professor Robert L. Leight, Ed.D.; Professor James Andrews; and Mr. Joseph Manusov, who read the manuscript, challenged ideas, suggested points for analysis, and made critical comments at various stages of the writing. The Reverend Keith J. Hardman deserves special mention, not only as a helpful reader and critic but also as the compiler of the index.

As always, special thanks are due those who live and work close to the writer, mostly for their patience and understanding.

W. B. W.

Ursinus College
Collegeville, Pennsylvania

Contents

CHAPTER I

Introduction

THIS VOLUME has a single purpose: to offer a philosophical critique of the theoretical foundations and of the major substantive and theological decisions from which Christian education derives its theory and program. A careful analysis of the philosophical foundations of this special field of education will explore and in part explicate the separate areas of philosophy and education and their confluence in the unique concerns of Christian education, especially in its claims to be a field capable of epistemological and definitional integrity and justification.

Part One will be concerned with broad questions dealing with the basic tasks and assumptions of philosophy, Christian education, and epistemology. In Parts Two and Three a philosophical critique will be made of decisions to "meet needs" and to emphasize "experience," of the theological commitments to "relationship theology" and "redemptive fellowship," and of the methodological decisions for unique "teaching" and "learning" theories, "custom-made" curricula and "local-option" methodology. The burden of these sections is to assay the language that the theorists of Christian education claim to be using. The need for this effort is thus seen to be the uncertainties and flaws in the actual theoretical foundations on which Christian education and curricular decisions are based.

It will not be the intention of this critique to hold that religious commitments and the ensuing language are nonsense. On the contrary, historical religious concepts are accepted in their proper context and honored for accomplishing the functional task prescribed by the context. For members of the faith community, statements involving that faith and its extension into life are not questionable until such statements are seen to be intended for the public community and to carry evaluations and prescriptions appealing to the wider realm of common or standard use.

In the case of the Christian education theorists in question the important issue to be analyzed is, What do the philosophical decisions communicate, and to which audience—fellow believers or the general community of rational men? Certainly, the language is hardly factual/empirical, although in the case of the two concepts of "needs" and "experience" such an inference is drawn. Further, the language is hardly confessional, for it carries recommendations to action and policy procedures. No, the language of Christian education is heavily evaluative and prescriptive. And even though couched in descriptive and informative-looking format, on analysis, the use is observed to shift from the empirical use to the special function the theorists prescribe. R. D. Heim, in his chapter in M. J. Taylor (ed.), *Religious Education*, supports my choice of concepts for analysis. He notes that a dozen of the principal concepts of the literature of the last decade include "church as 'redemptive community,' education within relationships, group dynamics, interpersonal relationships, needs of persons, confrontation with the gospel, [and] the 'drama of redemption.' "[1]

Of course, Christian education is heir not only to the body of thought and practices of the one parent discipline, education, but also to the vagueness and ambiguity of such educational terms as "integrated," "the whole person," "holistic," "child-centered," "nuclearity," and so on. And while it may seem to the uncritical that such ordinary words used in everyday speech are not at all obscure, yet it is highly doubtful that a clear, widely accepted use of any of the terms could be agreed upon by professional educators. Someone has said, "Once a cliché is in their heads, not even experience, let alone argument, will get it out again." Indeed, serious educational disputes have been provoked, and programs based on slogans vigorously attacked or defended, in both cases because of failure to analyze or clarify the factual and recommending educational statements.

It is at this point that philosophical analysis can perform an indispensable service—to elucidate the special language used in educational discourse. B. O. Smith and R. H. Ennis suggest that the essays in the trailblazing work which they edited, *Language and Concepts in Education,* "are intended to serve the following purposes":

1. To discover the neglected meanings which particular educational terms and expressions are given through the ways they are used in different contexts.
2. To uncover conceptual blunders and to lay bare erroneous lines of reasoning which result from failure to understand how language is being used in a given situation.
3. To clear away pseudo-problems and pseudo-questions that exist only as a result of confused and unclear conceptions, and the vague, ambiguous use of language.
4. To explore the dimensions of educational terminology and to gain a clearer understanding of the relationships between thought, language, and reality, and thus to broaden the basis upon which we ground our beliefs about reality and our convictions of value.
5. To lay bare unrecognized logical inconsistencies which result from the uncritical use of language.[2]

Part One will attempt to lay the proper foundation for the use of philosophy as a tool in the service of Christian education and at the same time apply the above purposes of language analysis. The importance of definition and conceptual clarity will be illustrated in the foundational chapters. Since they ask the right questions for definition and verifiability of knowledge, the philosophic task will be well illustrated even though the analysis and argument presented may be less than convincing and not at all constructive. With H. S. Smith, whose critique *Faith and Nurture* shocked many of his colleagues, this writer "believes that the present situation calls less for construction than for unsparing criticism."[3]

Here will be found an examination of the concerns usually described under the title of the Christian philosophy of education, but I hasten to add, it will not *be* a Christian philosophy of education. Under the headings of two elemental questions —What is philosophy? and What is Christian education?—an attempt will be made to establish the usefulness of philosophy as a tool in education, both secular and church, as well as to provide a careful evaluation of the definitions and objectives of that phenomenon called Christian education. Also included in this section is what I believe to be the first thorough study of the epistemological validity of Christian education. The various theories of knowledge will be discussed and some of the inadequacies and downright errors of several theorists will be considered and evaluated.

Part Two is a philosophical critique of four major substantive decisions or commitments crucial to much of modern Christian education. It will combine the techniques of a literary critique with those of philosophical analysis. A critique is a critical analysis or examination of a production, from a work of art to a specific institution. It is an evaluation of the ideas and concepts expressed in the work, as well as of the vehicle itself, in the light of a predetermined standard of values. Further, a critique also should report the excellences or faults of a work, indicating the criteria for the judgments expressed. Therefore, since by definition a critique involves scrutiny of the key ideas of a work and an appraisal of them, what follows in Part Two will be a scrutiny of four key concepts of several church educational theorists and an evaluation of the theoretical success each has achieved. No petty challenge of or to any party or designation is made herein, for instance, traditionalism vs. liberalism; nor is any specific pragmatic concern about mechanics or methods brought into question. The chief thrust of this analysis is to examine the decisions that have been most influential in formulating, prescribing, and defending church educational policy.

Two of the key terms are, in their standard use, neutral terms, which in comparably neutral contexts would have specific meaning and function. By neutral I mean that the terms are not laden with philosophical connotations. These words are "needs" and "experience." It will be demonstrated, however, that in wide contemporary usage both words shift from the standard secular function to a rather special function based largely, in the case of "needs," on a built-in prescriptivity, and, in the case of "experience," on a singular nonstandard use of that word meaning either "vicarious living" or simply "living through life."

The other key terms are "relationship theology" and "redemptive fellowship." There is little question here that both terms are philosophically laden. Both are being used in a nonneutral context and in an evaluative-prescriptive way in order to set or support an educational policy. In the case of "relationship" and "redemptive," as well as in the case of "needs" and "experience," the basic argument of the theorists is: "You ought to do X (educational task) because of: (1) the relationship factor involved; (2) the creation of a redemptive situation; (3) the scientifically discovered needs; or (4) the experience factor in the gathering together and the ongoing life of a church group."

Part Three will continue the procedure of Part Two and offer a philosophical critique of the methodological commitments of Christian education in both theoretical and technical areas. An analysis will be presented of the special decisions on "teaching" and "learning," curriculum definition and development, and the use made of these decisions in methodology. And, while this present study will be mostly concerned with conceptual analysis, it will be obvious that in methodological considerations pragmatic concerns are not easily put off or ignored. We will consider, therefore, both the language problem, i.e., Is the unique Christian educational "meaning" of the four educational concepts descriptive-empirical, or is it in fact highly prescriptive?; and the practical problem, i.e., Are the concepts as presented applicable to a general educational program?

Again, the three chapters that make up Part Three will examine and present a critique of the foundations literature of Christian education with emphasis on the theorists who were most influential in shaping church educational policies. The first two concepts are, in their usual use, reciprocal action terms dealing with a "doing" (of the teacher) and a "performance" (of the learner). In this usage they are nonphilosophical. However, I will show that in the Christian education usage "teaching" and "learning" shift from a rather neutral function to a special and *sui generis* function based on the prescriptivity of prior theological decisions.

The other two concepts, curriculum and methodology, are also nonphilosophical terms in the usual secular context. However, in church educational usage both terms shift from the rather neutral function to the special function dictated by theological purpose and prescription. The noneducational purposes that have motivated theorists will be shown to provide insubstantial foundations for educational curricula and methodology. And, while the justification of these positions and decisions is an appeal to "science"—the needs, experience, and religious issues of every age group—I will show, by reference to my analysis of these terms in Part Two, that slogans and theological prescriptions are no more "scientific" or reliable than the "traditional" bases for curricula and methodology that most modern theorists criticize.

The work will present, therefore, a general critique of Christian education in relation to the following specific questions:

1. What is philosophy and how can it be useful to a practical activity like Christian education?

2. What is Christian education and how does it function? Are its aims and objectives meaningful and productive?

3. Does Christian education apply and meet standard epistemological criteria? Is it important that it should?

4. How does the decision to "meet needs" function as used by the theorists? Does it furnish scientific data on which educational policy can be determined?

5. What does the term "experience" mean as used by the theorists? Can this meaning be taken as a foundation for educational policy?

6. What influence does the commitment to "relationship theology" have on the educational policy and curricular decisions?

7. What influence does the commitment to "redemptive fellowship" have on the educational policy and curricular decisions?

8. Is "Christian teaching" theoretically and practically meaningful? What does a teacher in the church do?

9. Is "Christian learning" a theory of learning in the usual educational sense or simply a promotional phrase?

10. Are the decisions to base curricula and methodology on theological purposes theoretical foundation enough to sustain a full educational program?

My primary purpose in offering this philosophical critique is simply to hold a critical mirror to the concepts reflected from the specific philosophical and methodological decisions of Christian education. I will try to note why these decisions were made and what they meant to the development of the educational policy and program of several Christian denominations in general and, especially, those churches considered the mainstream Protestant groups. I will not be concerned with debating the "big picture" in Christian educational theory, nor arguing the tenets of the competing, overarching metaphysical world views. I will offer no substitute theory or program. On the contrary, I will be concerned mostly with asking questions about the reasons for and the evidence behind the beliefs and opinions stated as justification for church educational concepts set forward as guides to the educational action.

My major philosophical concern is the identification of imprecision, vagueness, and ambiguity, even though it is readily admitted that some terms and concepts in religion are excused as essentially contentious and necessarily ambiguous. That is, those who use such terms and concepts prefer a certain fuzziness of language and indeed profit from the lack of clarity and thus avoid the confrontation of no-sense, contradiction, or failure to explain. Administrators in the field of Christian education are prone to use language that serves to advance practical activities in spite of the unrelieved theoretical confusion. As the author of *Theology in the New Curriculum* observed, "Vagueness is safe but ineffectual."[4]

The chapters that follow will not ring with positivism, optimism, and elegance. Indeed, they will be more likely to sound negative, pessimistic, and pedestrian. A Christian educator who read some of these pages remarked that after the last page he was ready to pick up the "positive thinking" of Norman Vincent Peale to get his perspective back. Nevertheless, a critique is what it is, and following the counsels of Ludwig Wittgenstein, who advocated the early and unsparing diagnosis of any disguised nonsense in language, as well as of C. G. Jung, who noted that only the meaningful sets men free, these pages will demand no less than clarity and sense in Christian education.

Philosophical Decisions

CHAPTER II

Philosophy and Christian Education

THE WORD "philosophy" appears often in the books and other materials enunciating the foundations of Christian education. It is used most often as a companion to the word "education," as in "philosophy of education," "educational philosophy," and "Christian philosophy of education." It is used, however, in many other ways, e.g., "philosophy of curriculum," "philosophy of wholeness," etc. Varied and non-technical uses of the word "philosophy" are quite common throughout the field of Christian education, where the word is taken to mean anything from "theory" to "general outlook," "presuppositions," and "practices."

The need for an examination of the use and misuse of the term is seen in the lament of W. N. Pittenger, a theologian-consultant to the Episcopal Church's Seabury Series, that a "distinguished expert in religious education frankly admitted in conversation that 'the whole philosophy upon which our practice has been based has been shown to be false, and we don't know what to do.' "[1] Also W. B. Kennedy, a Presbyterian educator and chronicler of the *Christian Faith and Life* curriculum, called for a book to be written in view of a "serious scarcity of materials dealing with a basic educational philosophy from the evangelical point of view, to express the point of view of the [new] curriculum."[2] He also tells of the victory of the theologians over professional educational "children's specialists" and noted that education had been forced into the role of "handmaiden."[3]

"What is philosophy itself? And what is the nature and function of the philosophical enterprise?" are said by J. H.

Randall to have been the subject of John Dewey's last discussion before the students at Columbia University. And what important questions they are! The first question has been tackled by many, for example, Elmer Sprague, who entitles his small but helpful book *What Is Philosophy?* The truth is that Sprague, like many others, rightfully turns from the first question to the second, or "What is the work of a philosopher?" Obviously, the latter question can be given an answer, for the work of philosophers is available for study and evaluation. Indeed, philosophy as a relevant discipline is a study of the opinions of past philosophers, as well as a searching criticism of their doctrines. D. J. O'Connor has thus characterized the philosophical function: "The student of philosophy learns . . . that he is not taught the opinions of Plato, Aristotle, Descartes and the rest because they are universally accepted as true. On the contrary, he finds that very few, if any, philosophical doctrines are generally held by philosophers and that he learns what Plato said about knowledge or what Descartes said about the relation between mind and body only, so it seems, to refute them. A large part . . . of philosophy consists in the destructive criticism of the opinions of the great philosophers from Socrates to Russell."[4]

Of course, for many the work of a philosopher traditionally could be described as a superior examination of life and the cosmos, which would result in the enunciation of an all-encompassing world view like that of Plato's theory of ideas, from which an explanation could be drawn of the nature of the universe, reality and being, knowledge, God, and human behavior. Further, philosophy as a "superior science" promised to produce answers to questions such as: What is truth? What can man know? What does the world contain? Does God exist? Is man free? What is right or wrong? And it promised to use rational procedures (sound argument) and grounds for support consistent with human reason. Unfortunately the task is just too great, and even a philosopher of rare metaphysical genius like Plato failed to measure up to the idea of philosophy as a "superior science." So often metaphysicians have provided doctrines not open to public verification and falsification, and to logical analysis by which philosophy becomes both a verifier and a clarifier of human knowledge and language.

As it seems that others have run into difficulties defining philosophy as a body of knowledge in itself, perhaps it might be described best by its function, namely, to use specific philosophic tools in the consideration of certain topics. Obviously, the first tool is that of observation and experience, by which the so-called "first-order" questions about that which is and that which happens in the world are verified (or falsified) by evidence.

The second tool is that of valid reason, which, while lacking a body of publicly testable knowledge, does help order the world and enable us to examine highly relevant questions and answers. Of course, reason can be misused as it was by the medievalists who believed it could prove anything. Still, if one follows Bertrand Russell, who defined a reasonable or rational man as "one who always proportioned the degree of intensity with which he held his various beliefs to the amount of evidence available for each belief,"[5] empiricism and rationalism can be employed together in the solution of philosophical questions. But the problem remains as to the evidence that is considered acceptable for nonscientific and nonmathematical questions, e.g., questions of morals, politics, and religion. Self-evident premises are doomed to failure on lack of evidence alone, although with John Wilson we must insist that evidence in metaphysical problems may be in the philosophical "in basket" awaiting appropriate discoveries and analysis.

The third tool of philosophy is language analysis, or, as Sprague says in defining the task of a philosopher, "straining what is said through a sieve that keeps back two kinds of talk: the nonsensical (yet to be given a sense or no-sense), and the self-contradictory (X is not X)."[6] Analytic philosophy is concerned with statements of empirical fact (verifiable as above by observation), with statements of logic (verifiable by coherence with a larger system of thought, e.g., mathematics), and with statements in ethics, aesthetics, politics, and religion, which are to be analyzed and criticized as a language use other than fact-stating. The important condition is to recognize the statement for what it is and what it is supposed to do. For instance, it is one thing to describe what is the case and another to prescribe what ought to be the case. The latter type of statement deals with "normative" questions and must be recognized not as fact-stating, but as value-stating, always a judgmental activity. Language analysis, therefore, examines meaning in use (connotation) and in application (denotation) in order to validate or invalidate second-order normative and religious statements.

Two more conditions can be mentioned. The first condition is that philosophy (defined by O'Connor as "a laborious, piece-meal effort to criticize and clarify the foundations of our beliefs"[7]) must not be the endorsement of any one more or less complete philosophical system, e.g., Platonism or existentialism. Since philosophy must be open to public testing, Platonism fails in the inaccessibility of the theory of ideas and existentialism is too private, mystical, and poetic to meet the test. System-building fails, in general, on the fatal illusion that there is such a thing as absolute, final, and certain knowledge, and that the entire system can be sustained deductively. The second condition is that in applying the tools of philosophy to other fields (especially to education), the philosopher will want to be familiar with the fields of metaphysics (What is the nature of reality?); ethics (What is right and good?); epistemology (What is knowledge? and How can it be gained?); and logic (What is the correct way of stating propositions?). The consideration of these questions or fields of traditional philosophy is essential to genuine inquiry into other disciplines.

Perhaps a word or two should be said on the importance of metaphysics, since with the rise of scientism and logical positivism it was "preached" that metaphysics was a waste of time. It is obvious that if metaphysics should try to maintain itself at the expense of science, it could readily be dismissed from consideration. However, more than one philosopher has acknowledged the dependence of science on metaphysics. Alfred

North Whitehead said, "No science can be more secure than the unconscious metaphysics which tacitly it presupposes."[8] It may be that a move to do away with metaphysics comes from a lack of understanding of metaphysical assumptions. There seems to be, as Russell notes, a "concealed metaphysics, usually unconscious in every writer on philosophy. . . . He is almost certain to have an uncritically believed system which underlies his explicit arguments."[9] Perhaps the greatest contribution of metaphysics to any field is the inevitable continuing discussion requiring thoughtful and patient treatment of problems that cannot be answered factually, and education is a field that is characterized by such questions.

James E. McClellan and B. Paul Komisar, in their preface to the American edition of C. D. Hardie's landmark in educational thought, *Truth and Fallacy in Educational Theory,* outline the role of philosophical analysis in education, admitting that "analysis is no single activity . . . [but] a cluster of activities, . . . [two of which] are elucidation and rational reconstruction . . . practiced upon concepts and theories."[10] In further developing their position, McClellan and Komisar answer charges leveled against the analyst. They admit, for instance, that some "vagueness and ambiguity in educational language . . . is itself functional . . . [in] performing its proper social role. This is certainly true of ceremonial utterances."[11] The authors admit also that "many of these services of analysis are patently prescriptive. . . . The point that beseeches attention is not whether analysis has a place in guiding and goading educational changes, but that anyone should ever have doubted it."[12] McClellan and Komisar also note, "It is the educator's mandate to culminate his work in recommendations."[13] Indeed, educational language without recommendations would be sterile and there is no harm whatsoever in voicing them, provided they are acknowledged for what they are and not played up as descriptive or scientific. Prescriptive or evaluative activity is the common aspect of both philosophy and education.

When we come to deal specifically with the term "philosophy

of education," we see that the ambiguity of meaning stems from an ambiguity in the meaning of the two major words themselves. Albert E. Best decries the use of the words together, regardless of their widespread usage in writings about the theory of education and formal instruction. O'Connor differentiates between what he calls "pretentious ["vague though high-sounding titles for miscellaneous talk about the aims and methods of teaching"] and muddle-headed [not always obvious what it means] use."[14]

Since the meaning of "philosophy" has been established above, no doubt an attempt to do the same for "education" would prove fruitful. One use of "education" is accepted by all—instruction in schools. But education is more than instruction or training in schools, and it is that something more which is usually considered the "wider meaning." O'Connor says education refers to:

(a) a set of techniques for imparting knowledge, skills and attitudes;
(b) a set of theories which purport to explain or justify the use of these techniques;
(c) a set of values or ideals embodied and expressed in the purposes for which knowledge, skills and attitudes are imparted and so directing the amounts and types of training that is given.[15]

Obviously the first two criteria, (a) and (b), are mostly factual and can be determined by the methods of science, after acknowledging the normative elements in both, to the satisfaction of most researchers. It is the empirical element in techniques and methodology that can be settled by observation and evidence. It is the recommending (normative) element in the case of "values or ideals" that is of dominant interest to the philosopher. Therefore, since the major questions of education are normative, they must be considered by the philosophy we have described above as the activity of criticism and clarification which can be directed against the statements of any discipline. Many would agree with O'Connor that "philosophy of education" should not be used unless it consider "those problems of philosophy which are of direct relevance to educational theory."[16]

Kingsley Price defines philosophy of education as "an analytical treatment of education together with an attempt to relate it in a certain way to metaphysics, ethics, and epistemology."[17] Any literature in educational theory must consider well Price's definition. Certainly the clarification by analysis of a number of obscure terms (jargon) in education is overdue, e.g., "the whole person," "integrated," etc. Metaphysics is germane to education in that it supplies explanation for statements in the factual part and notes what evidence is to be accepted, e.g., Thomism as the basic presupposition of Roman Catholic education. A concern for ethics and the nature of value judgments and the logic of their justification is for O'Connor the point of ultimate contact between education and philosophy. Indeed, philosophy of education "involves a serious study of moral philosophy as a whole."[18] Finally, education must depend on epistemology (theory of knowledge) to provide a relevant theory of learning and a program to secure learning in fact.

Of course, there will be those who object to such a limitation of the nature and task of philosophy, and also those who would remind me of the philosophers who continue to put together systems of thought and enunciate a world view complete enough to provide an answer to the main concerns of the history of philosophy. Further, there are those who hold that the words "philosophy of education" are taken to mean a system of practical methods in teaching based, not on empirically tested theory, but, as O'Connor described, on "guesses at explaining successful practice. Some of [these] were acute and systematic but mistaken like the psychology of Herbart. Some . . . [were] unsubstantiated conjecture, like Montessori's view on the training of the senses. Some, like Pestalozzi's doctrine of *Anschauung*, were unintelligible adaptations of metaphysical concepts."[19]

Pittenger illustrates the uncritical regard for "philosophy of education" as he observes that the difficulty in Christian education has been "a reliance on the whole point of view of 'progressive' education . . . [which] has held the entire teaching profession in captivity . . . and with . . . modifications and accommodations . . . much of religious education."[20] Like others, Pittenger wrongly blames John Dewey for this state of affairs, since the "progressive" movement adopted only Dewey's methods, but ignored his theories. Actually, for John Dewey, philosophy and education were virtually indistinguishable.

Examples of the misuse of the word "philosophy" in Christian education are numerous. V. O. Ward, Kennedy, and the Methodist pamphlet *Foundations of Christian Teaching in Methodist Churches,* speak of "the philosophy of the [Methodist] curriculum."[21] There is little doubt that "philosophy" to all three meant theories, presuppositions, or foundations, and they should have so written. Dorothy L. Braun, Episcopal educator and chronicler of the Seabury Series, observes that "the philosophy and method of the Seabury Series seems to have won many adherents. The weakness lies in the areas of not implementing the philosophy and method fully enough."[22] "Philosophy" here means commitments or assumptions, but perhaps the criticism in the second half of the statement means that the assumptions, commitments, and methodological decisions were advanced too timidly.

B. A. Yeaxlee remarks that "we find ourselves . . . working out . . . the philosophy of wholeness, . . . the only philosophy accordant with a Gestalt psychology." L. J. Sherrill also speaks of "a philosophy of wholeness," and E. F. Zeigler writes that "there is deep need . . . to establish some kind of working philosophy . . . in which the whole of life can be interpreted meaningfully."[23] Now, it may be that Zeigler has explained "the philosophy of wholeness" in his explication of a "working philosophy"; however, the phrase seems little more than a slogan suggesting that Christian education consider and deal with all areas of human and institutional life. Indeed, D. C. Wyckoff suggests that philosophy is "the highest intellectual function of the culture" as it answers the fundamental questions of existence, and Iris V. Cully adds that "philosophy has set as its task the probing of the depths of . . . environmental descriptions of man's existence."[24] In this use, "philosophy" must be read to mean "theology" or some type of religious metaphysics quite unavailable to the probing of philosophical inquiry. Of course, there is a popular use of the word "philosophy" obvious in all the news media, in speeches and sermons. However, a scholarly discipline, to which Christian education aspires, must demand more of its practitioners than popular and nontechnical language.

Analysis of the term "philosophy of education" has provided a basis for the more precise use of philosophical tools on educational issues, although it must be regretfully admitted that there are those who still recommend dealing with issues in education within the framework of a systematic philosophy, a grand system to avoid distortion and controversy.[25] The use of the term "philosophy of Christian education" can be allowed on the grounds that Christian educators do put educational questions to philosophy, seeking analytic, epistemological, metaphysical, and ethical answers. Christian education will achieve maturity and academic status as it merges analytic treatment of the educational effort of the Christian community with theological discourse to deal with the unsettled problems of epistemology, metaphysics, and ethics. The answer to the question, Is there a Christian philosophy of education? must be negative on the ground that there is no such thing as Christian mathematics, chemistry, or physics. As Paul Tillich so often pointed out, the term "Christian philosophy" is ambiguous. Further, such an appellation would inspire adherence to F. E. Gaebelein's claim that "nothing short of a philosophy centered in Biblical truth has a right to the name Christian."[26]

Numerous Christian educational theorists have sought to avoid what R. C. Miller identified as "the fundamental weakness in practically all educational theory; a failure to grasp the purpose of Christian education and to impart Christian truth. . . . Our philosophy of educational method has been sound at the expense of theology."[27] Sherrill concurs in stressing the importance of theology in Christian education and adds that "education can be based on a philosophy of encounter." And Howard Grimes remarks that his "purpose is to state a philosophy of Christian nurture consistent with [his] view of the Church" and calls for a reevaluation "in terms of both a theology and educational philosophy which are sound." Paul H. Vieth says, "Whatever is of central interest to the church [in theology] is also of interest to Christian education."

R. R. Boehlke moves one step beyond to urge that "learning theory insights . . . are to be utilized as servants of theology for the special concerns of the church." Cully observes that "any educational philosophy has a center. . . . The Church too has a center, . . . God"; therefore Christian education is "theocentric." Indeed, James D. Smart argues that "education, by its very nature, . . . has a religious significance and is based on theological presuppositions. . . . We must speak of the theological *character* of education."[28] Commentary is in order on the preceding points of view. One might expect such positions to be expressed in support of any kind of special education; unfortunately, most of these claims are either unsupported or unsupportable.

David R. Hunter rejects "philosophy of education," commenting in an interview that "no existing philosophy of education [by which he means systems of educational programs or slogans] is applicable to Christian education."[29] Hunter prefers "theology of education," which he says fits Christian educational presuppositions. He writes: "The theology of a Christian education program is determined by what it assumes about God, about the mission of the Church, and about salvation. . . . Much depends, therefore, on how seriously one takes the task of establishing the purpose of an educational program. . . . Engagement [an existentialist slogan] must be the immediate and the ultimate criterion . . . [with] its focus in what God is doing. . . . [The Church's] task is one of enabling man to respond [not particularly to understand] to what God is doing."[30]

Nels F. S. Ferré also supports "the term 'Christian theology of education' . . . to preclude . . . diluting . . . the faith . . . in some alien philosophy like idealism . . . or pragmatism . . .

using Biblical and historical data for its basis. . . . Christian philosophers . . . have been convinced . . . that Christ is the truth for both life and education. Christian education will do well to follow their roads."[31]

Miller develops this concept even further in his *Clue to Christian Education*. His "clue" is *not* to put theology at the center of the curriculum. This spot is reserved for an encounter or a twofold relationship between God and the learner. "No," Miller says, "theology must be prior to the curriculum [because] theology is 'truth-about-God-in-relation-to-man.' . . . [But] the task of Christian education is not to teach theology, but to use theology as the basic tool for bringing learners into the right relationship with God in the fellowship of the Church. . . . [Yet] this does not mean that we can be dogmatic about it."[32]

Smart acknowledges Miller's "clue" to Christian education, i.e., "that theology has been the missing element," but he takes issue with Miller's assumption "that the existing educational structure needs only to have a satisfactory theology inserted beneath it and it will be securely founded." Smart continues: "At no point does he [Miller] take account of the actual situation: that the Church's educational program already has, not only beneath it but involved in every detail of it, a number of theologies, and that, because Christian educators have failed to be critical theologians, the Church has lacked a department of theology that would help it, in its educational activities, to escape from false or confused theologies into a true theology. The problem is far too great and complicated to yield to any facile solution."[33] Of course, Smart's critique of Miller is sound; however, his proposal fails at the same point as the Hunter-Ferré-Miller move to avoid the philosophical anxieties of proper "philosophy of education," i.e., What is a "true" theology?

In each case many more analytical problems are posed. A complete retreat from the arena of analysis is apparent. These theorists have forsaken "philosophy of education" for "theology" (defined by Miller as "truth-about-God-in-relation-to-man"), the "theology of a Christian education program" (defined by Hunter as "engagement, what God is doing and man's response"), and "Christian theology education" (defined by Ferré as "the use of Biblical and historical data," and by Smart as "true theology"). They have chosen to base church educational programs on religious decisions far removed from public verification. Further, Wyckoff has pointed out that as yet, "there is no 'theology of education,' . . . no 'Christian philosophy of education,' . . . nor any other specifically Christian disciplinary analysis. It is the task of Christian education theory . . . to work at this matter."[34]

It is obvious to me that Christian educators, much like many of their counterparts in general education, have misused "philosophy," or at best, they have been satisfied to accept the man-in-the-street usage of "philosophy," as a special view of things that will solve all questions. While I do not eschew the discussion of the great questions of man, I do prefer that any discussion of epistemology, metaphysics, and ethics be pursued with the most precise use of every philosophical tool in a dogged analysis of the statements made to accomplish fullest elucidation and, when necessary, rational reconstruction of the argument. The adoption of such a use of "philosophy" has already been of benefit to general education in the clarification of otherwise obscure terms and the unsparing critique of the recommending and normative elements. Obviously a similar application of philosophical analysis would be a boon to Christian education. It remains to be seen if the theorists and theologians will accept the brutal scrutiny of open philosophical criticism or claim the exemption of an "otherwordly" language inaccessible to public examination.

CHAPTER III

What Is Christian Education?

IN A SPECIAL thirty-fifth anniversary issue, the *International Journal of Religious Education* devoted more than half its space to an examination of the concept under the general title "What Is Christian Education?" In the introduction the editorial board admitted candidly that they "did not find it easy to describe Christian education." They further admitted that what they were offering was an "interpretation . . . given with no illusion as to its adequacy, but in the hope that it will help *all* . . . come to a clear understanding of the role of . . . [and a] clear picture of what Christian education is."[1] Unfortunately, in spite of the abundance of articles on the various aspects of religious education, e.g., teaching and learning, a workable definition of the concept is just not available. As a matter of fact, near the conclusion of the editorial, the editors admit that " 'What is Christian education?' is an open-end question."[2]

Surely there is a clear and unambiguous answer! I once thought so, as I wrote in *A Handbook for Episcopalians*: "Christian education . . . is a system of teaching set in the framework of the Christian faith."[3] However, as bland as my definition is, I now agree with Grimes, who says that "to attempt a definition is to risk being presumptuous."[4]

Another emphasis of the *Journal* was on the aims or tasks (also called objectives or goals) of Christian education, an emphasis that mirrors the universal concern for an answer to the companion question, What are the aims of Christian education? Zeigler speaks for all Christian educators as he notes, "Goals help us to know and see where we are headed; only by setting goals can we hope to achieve success."[5] The International Council of Religious Education report supports the

importance of aims: "Objectives . . . determine the direction
which the educational process will take, . . . the types of experience that are to be selected and used in developing the
curriculum, . . . the methods and the materials to be used, . . .
and . . . [the] basis on which to evaluate the results of the
program."[6]

There is no dearth of either definitions or statements of aims,
yet, as Wilson points out in his article in *Aims in Education,*
questions like, What is Christian education? and What are the
aims of Christian education? are often a waste of the question-
er's time, because, as Wilson suggests: "They are an excuse for
the person who answers them to put forward various opinions
of his own as if they constituted the only true answer; and as
any philosopher will tell you, there cannot be *a* true answer
to such questions, because they are not true questions. . . . You
might be asking for a dictionary [or stipulative] definition . . .
or for a sociological account of the causes of existing . . .
processes, or for someone's opinion about what these processes
ought to be, or for practically anything."[7] However, since
"everybody's doing it," this critique must examine the questions
asking for definition and aims, as well as the discussion attending the answers; for while imprecise, clumsy, and muddled
language causes the philosopher no end of concern, the practical application of the general principles enunciated in the
course of our attempt brands the inquiry as no waste of
time.

Perhaps an examination of some of the many definitions of
Christian education culled from the works of numerous theorists will reveal the folly of expecting clear, unambiguous
definition. The only definition offered in the *Journal*'s special
issue is given by Alva I. Cox, Jr.: "Christian education is the
process of communicating the Christian gospel to others in
such a way that all of life is surrendered to the lordship of
Christ," or it is helping persons "accept the Christian faith
not only as intellectual assent to formal theological propositions, but as the active living out of that faith in the experiences
of their common life."[8] Others say that Christian education is:

1. The attempt . . . to participate in and to guide the changes which take place in persons in their relationships with God, with the church, with other persons, with the physical world, and with oneself. . . . [Also] certain significant aspects of the dynamics of interaction in the Christian community. (Sherrill)[9]

2. The ministry of instruction [for the experience of growth], carried on by both the language of words and the language of relationship. . . . [It] must be personal, . . . a divine-human encounter . . . [and] is responsible for the . . . transmission of the subject matter (the recital of God's saving acts). (Howe)[10]

3. A particular type of relationship between two or more human beings, a relationship characterized by one of these human beings having as his intention the aiding of the other in gaining an authentic self, i.e., accepting his self as a gift for which he is responsible to the Father. . . . This type of relationship . . . we call pedagogic. (Paddock)[11]

4. The point at which God and man enter a renewed personal relationship within a community of persons. . . . [Also learning] the Gospel of redemption . . . by sharing the redeeming relationships within a [Christian] community. (Miller)[12]

5. Interested in re-creating personality, reconstructing personality, and transforming personality. . . . Personality configurations . . . must be taken as indicative of ways in which the individual can develop and ways . . . to provide the experiences through which he may come into full and abundant Christian living. (Wyckoff)[13]

6. The development by human means of human capacities for religious [Christian] response to the demands of life . . . [with the additional note that] everything that happens in a parish educates people. (Crawford)[14]

7. Spiritual nurture because it is training in spiritual relationship through spiritual relationships. . . . [It] is not so much *what* is done on certain occasions as it is a *way* of doing everything on all occasions. (Rummer)[15]

8. Communicating the gospel, . . . a function of the Church whereby the *laos* are nurtured, taught, trained and otherwise equipped for their day-by-day ministry in God's world, . . .

for life and work in the whole human family. (*Workbook: Developing Your Educational Ministry*)[16]

9. An effective medium through which the Holy Spirit creates and nurtures Christian persons, . . . a process in which persons are confronted with and . . . transformed by the Christian Gospel, and led into and nurtured within the Church. (*The Objectives of Christian Education*)[17]

A close examination of the several definitions posed shows up the difficulty involved in expecting a single clear and true answer to the question, What is Christian education? While all definitions were written by "experts" in religious education, they do not yield a unified answer nor indeed even a broadly homogeneous one. Cox suggests a noneducational result, "a surrender" to be achieved through communicating the "gospel," which might well be shown to be a psychological and not a logical "process." Sherrill's definition includes the concept of learning as change, but it lapses into "relationship" ambiguity and also seems to emphasize psychological slogans which themselves await definition. Howe, while admitting to a responsibility for transmitting the subject matter, tailors his definition to the proportion of his theological commitment—a commitment to existentialism and relationship theology. Paddock seems hardly to be describing an educational activity in any ordinary sense even though he labels it "pedagogic."

Miller also takes the relationalist road, but the question remains, Is what he is describing education or learning in ordinary language? Or is he joining slogans in line with his theological commitment? Wyckoff is simply guilty of pedagogical overload. Christian education has its limitations, and "re-creating personality" must lie beyond these limits. Crawford's definition is simply nonsense. Rummer is indulging in circularity and joins Crawford in his "*way* of doing everything" to say nothing. The Methodist *Workbook* assumes a result of unbelievable proportions "equipped for . . . ministry," and the words "nurtured," "taught," and "trained" keep the definition imprecise. The Lutheran *Objectives of Christian Education* is a standard churchly appeal to a divine process with the

Holy Spirit as creator and teacher of Christians. At best, this must be accepted as symbolic or ceremonial language and not available for philosophic inquiry.

Obviously, therefore, all that can be said in answer to the question, What is Christian education? is that Christian groups do organize their resources and personnel for an activity or program often described as instruction in content material selected as important and relevant to the particular Christian group, with appropriate methods and for purposes and ends designated by the group. Further, it can be said that the many answers proposed by "experts" in Christian education are in the nature of both an apologetic for the church's decisions and an exhortation to the members to go along with the programs. And certainly there are some "experts" who voice little more than their own opinions, religious points of view, and educational slogans in their answers.

As the examination of several definitions revealed the folly of the task, perhaps a look at a few statements of aims will expose the fruitlessness of aims-setting in Christian education. Actually, every theorist has aims/goals/objectives/purposes to propose, and aims statements are available from every Christian body, as well as from national and international councils. The International Council of Religious Education has formulated the following statement of objectives:

   I. Christian education seeks to foster in growing persons a consciousness of God as a reality in human experience, and a sense of personal relationship to him.

  II. Christian education seeks to develop in growing persons such an understanding and appreciation of the personality, life and teaching of Jesus as will lead to experience of him as Savior and Lord, loyalty to him and his cause, and will manifest itself in daily life and conduct.

 III. Christian education seeks to foster in growing persons a progressive and continuous development of Christlike character.

 IV. Christian education seeks to develop in growing persons the ability and disposition to participate in and contribute constructively to the building of a social order throughout the world, embodying the ideal of the Fatherhood of God and the brotherhood of man.

V. Christian education seeks to develop in growing persons an appreciation of the meaning and importance of the Christian family, and the ability and disposition to participate in and contribute constructively to the life of this primary social group.

VI. Christian education seeks to develop in growing persons the ability and disposition to participate in the organized society of Christians—the Church.

VII. Christian education seeks to lead growing persons into a Christian interpretation of life and the universe; the ability to see in it God's purpose and plan: a life philosophy built on this interpretation.

VIII. Christian education seeks to effect in growing persons the assimilation of the best religious experience of the race, preeminently that recorded in the Bible, as effective guidance to present experience.[18]

The Lutheran Church has announced in a brief statement the general objectives for Christian education:

"Inasmuch as the Church, as the Body of Christ, seeks to become more effectively that community of believers in which the Holy Spirit calls, gathers, enlightens, and sanctifies individuals in their relationships with God and their fellow men, the Church's central educational objective, therefore, shall be—

"To assist the individual in his response and witness to the eternal and incarnate Word of God as he grows within this community of the church toward greater maturity in his Christian life through ever-deepening understandings, more wholesome attitudes, and more responsible patterns of action."[19]

And The Methodist Church has adapted the following objective from the National Council of Churches: "That all persons be aware of and grow in their understanding of God, especially of his redeeming love as revealed in Jesus Christ, and that they respond in faith and love—to the end that they may know who they are and what their human situation means, increasingly identify themselves as sons of God and members of the Christian community, live in the spirit of God in every relationship, fulfill their common discipleship in the world, and abide in the Christian hope."[20]

Other theorists say that the aim of Christian education is:

1. Discipleship, . . . nurturing and equipping every member to participate responsibly in the fulfillment of the church's mission, . . . making its program as effective as possible so that all may know, accept [and] follow Christ. (*Christian Education in Our Church*)[21]

2. To nurture and train the members of the parish of all ages through worship and encounter with the meaning of the Gospel for their lives, that they may *live gloriously* and carry on the mission of the Church in all situations. (*A Guide for Selecting Curriculum Materials*)[22]

3. To remake, remold, transform, and reconstruct the experience of the children, youth, and adults with whom we live and work that they will experience their lives as the life in Christ. (Wyckoff)[23]

4. To lead the child to a vital experience of God, to rediscover the experience of transcendence. . . . Our duty lies in helping children to retain and develop their natural powers of religious perception. . . . The achievement of the aim . . . is to bridge the gap between revelation and "response-ability." (Chaplin)[24]

5. That persons might be drawn into the kingdom of God; that they might attain to increasing self-understanding and self-knowledge and an increasing realization of their own potentialities; and that they might sustain the relationships and responsibilities of life as children of God. (Sherrill)[25]

6. To help people gain a right relationship to God and to all men . . . [and] Christian maturation. . . . It [maturation] can involve nothing less than finding God as the total context of meaning and the final end for motivation. . . . Salvation is a matter of right *total* relation to God. (Ferré)[26]

7. Not merely the imparting of religious knowledge; it is also the work of building Christian community within which both verbal language and the language of relationships mutually reinforce each other in communicating the gospel of reconciliation and hope to man in his estrangement and despair. (Ernsberger)[27]

A cursory analysis of these several statements of aims for Christian education will justify Wilson's demur regarding the impossibility of a request for an answer to "What are the aims of Christian education?" Indeed, R. S. Peters decries any attempt to talk of aims in education, since the so-called aims are "neither goals nor . . . end-products, [but] ways of talking about doing some things rather than others and doing them in a certain manner . . . [or] principles implicit in different manners of proceeding or producing."[28]

The classical statement of objectives from the International Council of Religious Education is composed of statements vague enough to allow all the really interesting disputes in theology to slip by, e.g., "to foster in growing persons a consciousness of God as a reality in human experience." Of course, this observation is significant in the examination of all aims statements, but its basis is not accessible to standard verification procedures. The Lutheran statement is oriented to an otherworldly source of education, but it does mention human assistance and results. The Methodists follow the pattern, but add relationalist jargon and the interesting noneducational goal to "know who they are." The Presbyterians set as a single objective "discipleship," which when explained enlarges the task beyond the limitations of human education—"the fulfillment of the church's mission."

The Episcopal statement seems to have little concern with any educational processes at all. Of course the goal of living "gloriously" *is* a challenge! Wyckoff again poses an impossible task for education. His verbs give him away: "remake," "remold," "transform," and "reconstruct." And his result escapes any known "experience"—"that they will experience their lives as *the life in Christ*" (my emphasis). Chaplin also uses ordinary words strangely: "lead," "experience," "natural powers," "perception," in a way that renders them unavailable to analysis. Sherrill has posed aims that are little more than an exhortation based on his religious opinions (self-knowledge as a goal) and theological commitments (relationship). Ferré and Ernsberger also combine relationship theology and a bit of existentialism as a way of proceeding in Christian education. Ferré's call to "right *total* relation to God" as giving meaning and motivation is "disguised nonsense." And Ernsberger's popular ploy regarding knowledge of, but not about, God is homiletical nonsense.

Nevertheless, definitions and aims statements will continue to be made in Christian education and will continue to be printed and circulated among the "faithful" who follow the theorists and their esoteric writings. Indeed, it is the intramural aspect of the talk among the "specialists" in Christian education that prompted Sherrill to explode "an official class of clergymen and other highly trained church workers who gradually come to form a self-conscious caste of professional religionists. These people speak a sort of professional religious jargon peculiar to themselves but not fully understood by other people. Gradually they lose touch . . . and come to be regarded as a kind of . . . union . . . of religious experts, without whom . . . the work of the church cannot go on— . . . shrewd demagogues who know how to use religious slogans with a powerful effect."[29]

Slogans and slogan systems in education and the several special adhering educational areas have a special appeal and use, but they are of untold importance in definitional and aims statements. While the obvious use of slogans is ceremonial and emotional, arousing interest, enthusiasm, and motivation, and while such slogans are unlike definitions or generalizations, which are usually descriptive in nature, implying a (defined) set of characteristics, there is a usage that is analogous to definitions. Such slogans begin as rallying words in a speech or an article and end up as the symbol of a movement and are interpreted quite literally. This was true of Dewey and "progressive education." He coined the slogans and his followers turned them into applied slogan systems, e.g., "learn by experience." In Christian education entire programs of education have been built on a slogan. For instance, "wholeness" or the "whole person" has been enlarged to include the holistic psychology, method, and ministry. And such vague and ambiguous concepts as "the real self," "self-knowledge," and "becoming," as well as the notions of "beginning where a man is," "nuclear function," and "existential situation," all qualify as nondescriptive slogans and slogan systems. They are all prescriptive and recommend, advise, or exhort our action predetermined for us by the definers and aims makers who decide what our behavior and feelings should be, and then plan the manipulative program accordingly.

One question remains: Is Christian education indoctrination? Of course, the traditionalist answer is yes, and much of the history of Christian education offers evidence to support the claim for indoctrination. Indeed, the universal church can hardly be said to do anything other than indoctrinate. Yet Dryden voices our concern:

> By education most have been misled;
> So they believe, because they were so bred.
> The priest continues what the nurse began,
> And thus the child imposes on the man.[30]

Smart notes that "all teaching involves a danger of some measure of coercive indoctrination, but we do not for that reason abandon our schools and colleges that our children may be free to discover the truth for themselves."[31] And Sherrill criticizes those who are fearful of indoctrination, saying, "They have felt it necessary to indulge in all sorts of methodological devices so as to skirt around frankly giving instruction."[32]

Wilson makes a point for some differentiation on the basis of content of education, noting that subjects with uncertain beliefs (politics, morals, and religion) seem to lend themselves to indoctrination. Wilson points out that there is little publicly accepted evidence in the uncertain subjects, ruling out "what the sectarians like to consider evidence." He further comments that "the metaphysical and moral beliefs are uncertain in a deeper sense. . . . We do not know what sort of evidence to look for." The proper function of education is to clarify and interpret reality, whereas indoctrination "begins when the behavior we teach children is . . . demanded by ourselves and not by reality at all."[33] Richard M. Hare, also a contributor to *Aims in Education,* adds another criterion to the indoctrination discussion as he notes that purpose must be considered. If the purpose of an institution is, in fact, to teach a specific religion with specific doctrines in a specific way, it is quite likely the process can be called indoctrination.

What my thesis means for Christian education is simply this: admit with the author of *Parent-Parish Program* that "the question is not whether a child shall be religious, but what kind of religion will dominate him";[34] acknowledge the special nature of the educational program necessary in the Christian church; and plan the program accordingly. If we accept Wilson's analysis, religion does not fit his categories of evidence and "a democratic exchange of views"; therefore, the test of rationality will not apply and Christian education is seen to be indoctrination in the literal sense of the word. The meaning of "indoctrination" (from *doctrinaire*, to teach or instruct, and *doctrina*, learning) is "instruction in the rudiments and principles of any science," or "to imbue with a doctrine (or beliefs)." Thus, it is obvious that Christian education *does* aim at establishing certain beliefs and that while some theorists would wish such beliefs to be held as though they were arrived at through experimental and empirical methods, full inquiry and weighing of evidence is not possible in Christian education, at least until after a certain body of belief is mastered. Wide-ranging discussion and a free exchange of views will then be possible. Indeed, most churches feel it mandatory to instruct their young in "correct" beliefs and a way of life established thereon.

W. R. Niblett soundly supports the indoctrination thesis in Christian education. "I believe that we are not only thoroughly justified in biasing and influencing our children . . . but it is our absolute obligation to do so. . . . We must not be afraid of educating for commitment."[35] The church, since it does demand commitment to a specific set of beliefs and a certain type of moral behavior, can hardly be faulted for planning to educate for that commitment. As Aristotle remarked, "It is therefore not of small importance whether we are brought up from childhood in one set of habits or another; on the contrary, it is of very great, or rather of supreme importance."[36]

CHAPTER IV

Epistemology and Christian Education

NO PROGRAM of education, no matter what its orientation or designation, is exempt from describing and developing a theory of knowledge. Indeed, since the discovery and the transmission of knowledge is the prime concern of education, the analysis of knowledge and the grounds for knowledge demand a consideration of the special field of philosophy in which such analyses are made—epistemology.

Unfortunately, very few of the theorists in Christian education engage in epistemological inquiry specifically, although it is indirectly considered in formulations of theological and faith foundations or implied in an analysis of learning. A thorough research of many books, pamphlets, and articles reveals not only that epistemology is not a live issue but also that the word is not often used. Some Christian educators object that as "specialists" they have a practical job to do—the day-by-day task of implementing the educational mission of the church. But how unfortunate is this neglect of theoretical discussion and crucial investigation of philosophical foundations, in view of the dependence on "practical" teaching, learning, curriculum, and methodology on theoretical and substantive decisions. It is for this reason that epistemological analysis of issues in the general theory of knowledge against the educational background of the Christian religion is important to Christian education.

Epistemology has been called the most exacting and difficult field of philosophy and the "inspector general" of philosophy, since it seeks to examine the structure, methods, and validity of knowledge. For many philosophers, this examination is of the intellectual equipment of humans and the guarantee to "know" implicit in the statements that we make. Our concern at this point is for answers to the questions: What can we know? How can we know? and What are the ways we can be said to know? Of course, there is an ordinary use of "know" which can be used to answer the questions: being familiar with objects, learning something, and believing something to be true. However, a more exact use of "know" is necessary to a discussion of educational theory. To "know" in a precise way is to: (1) determine what the question is; (2) decide how to verify its validity; (3) decide what evidence will verify or falsify; and (4) determine belief.

Sprague has suggested that a consideration of the "ways" of knowing leads through an analysis of "knowledge as declarative statements [words designed to do a specific language job], which someone knows how to prove or to use."[1] He identifies two kinds of knowledge: matters of fact "which depend on man's sense, or his powers of perceiving; and matters of logic [called by Hume "relation of ideas"] which depend on man's reason or his powers of conceiving."[2] To this discrimination, I have added a third kind—matters of appraisal, which depend on a man's point of view or personal commitment.

Matter-of-fact statements are called descriptive, informative, and empirical in philosophical literature, but regardless of label, we are discussing scientific knowledge, perceptual in nature, dependent on the senses, and verifiable by observation and experience. Matter-of-logic statements are also called analytical, logical, and definitional, but with them we are presenting conceptual knowledge, dependent on mental powers, reason, and ideas, and verifiable by coherence to a larger system of thought or "truth by definition." Matter-of-appraisal statements are made mostly in areas of contested knowledge, e.g., religion, morals and all values, politics, education, and human relations. And while appraisal or assessment statements contain both factual and logical elements, they are mainly evaluative, prescriptive, or emotive, and are verified from a point of view or a chosen decision.

Matter-of-fact statements have an immediate appeal in that they are verifiable by direct observation and human experience and that they have science as a model. The world view (or metaphysic) most closely aligned with matters of fact is empiricism, which accepts as "real" only that knowledge which comes from and is verified by the senses. We know what we can see, hear, smell, taste, feel, as observed facts. And while it is true that senses sometimes deceive (e.g., the stick observed to be bent in water), nevertheless, the so-called one-to-one correspondence of fact to fact remains the most respected truth theory in modern secular education.

Matter-of-logic statements do not describe or give information about the world, but help to order it, and mathematics is the model. We accept or reject analytical statements based on either the logical or intelligible way the statement is used or by an appeal to human reason. Those who stress analytical statements are known as rationalists. Rationalism's truth claims are based on logical or mathematical relations and a certain self-consistency as well as on the use of reason to interpret and synthesize perceptions of fact. Of course, if reason has no balance in fact, it will reflect Kant's classical criticism of rationalism that "concepts without percepts are empty." But Kant also pointed out that "percepts without concepts are blind," and argued for the interdependence of reason and sense perception in the pursuit of knowledge. However, with Sprague, we must recognize the limitation of matter-of-logic statements in that they "tell us nothing of existence."[3] Indeed, language does not entail existence, and no conclusions of reality can be drawn from language.

Matter-of-appraisal statements are the main interest of modern philosophy, since they are made on the basic human questions in ethics, religion, aesthetics, politics, education, and human relations. Of course, where possible, philosophers turn to natural science or mathematics and logic for solutions, but generally the answers are either elusive or just not there. The philosopher is thus thrown back upon the use of reason and dialogue or inquiry to determine the grounds for systematically contested ethical, religious, aesthetical, political, educational, and sociological knowledge. The admissibility of evidence is part of the contest and the decision often is made under objection. But with Russell, all philosophers hope that beliefs concerning the basic human questions will be based in their intensity on the amount of evidence available.

Sprague differentiates between matters of fact and logic as "between what is in the world [a matter of fact] and what is in my mind [as a concept or as someone's knowing how to use a word],"[4] which is a matter of logic. Matters of appraisal are conceptual, of course, but they are uniquely different from fact and logic in their appeal to evaluation, faith, and point of view with little or no dependence upon the scientific method or mathematical and logical consistency. Of course, in all three to "know" means quite simply "support what you claim to know properly." Israel Scheffler holds that "'knowing that' attributions reflect the truth judgments and critical standards of the speaker; and they hinge on the particular criteria of backing for beliefs, which he adopts," and that to "know" is having a belief which a man considers within himself, in Augustine's words, "whether it is true."[5]

There are other kinds of truth or knowledge theories—intuitivism, pragmatism, and authoritarianism—and some would add skepticism, although the skeptic argues that genuine knowledge is unattainable. The intuitivist bases his truth criteria on intuition or "self-evident statements," which Sprague defines as those "which someone agrees to as soon as he understands . . . [their] terms."[6] It is probably the most personal way of knowing. G. F. Kneller declares that intuitivism is "ultimately connected with feeling and contrasts with the logical processes usually connected with thinking at the conscious level."[7] Often intuitive explanations mention "mystical experience" ("I saw or heard God last night") or just "insight," referring to a sudden apprehending of knowledge. Obviously, intuition alone can hardly be considered a unique source of knowledge. It must be balanced by the concepts of reason and the percepts of the senses mentioned above. Nevertheless, J. S.

Bruner has called intuition "an essential feature of productive thinking, not only in formal academic circles, but also in everyday life."[8]

The pragmatist or instrumentalist holds what Kneller calls "probably the most widely held theory of knowledge in educational circles today,"[9] that the best way to discover knowledge is to make a statement and then test its practical effectiveness or utility in use. As Kneller points out: "Man does not simply receive knowledge; he makes it. . . . Knowledge is a *transaction* between man and his environment."[10] The problem is not just Does it work? but rather, as Dewey proposed, that in an attempt to clear up a problematic situation man must engage in a method of inquiry (the "scientific method") consisting of investigation of data, hypothesis making, and testing. As H. S. Broudy describes it, "On the Instrumentalist view, truth *means* a matching of what one predicts will be the case and what turns out to be the case."[11] Pragmatism is actually empiricism with a thorough grounding in the "coordinate" relationship of the material world and the intelligent, human organism.

Authoritarianism is another type of truth or knowledge theory. Authoritative knowledge depends on an individual or an institution or upon the social experience of mankind usually stored up in books. Even though we unconsciously reject the concept of authority, especially the authority of a dictator, we nonetheless depend for knowledge almost exclusively upon the experience of our social group. Transmitted by the process of education, authority does provide stability and shortcuts in our endless quest for knowledge. Of course, in the fields of science, mathematics, etc., we can always check the truth of factual knowledge, and where necessary replace old information with new. And in the fields of ethics, religion, politics, and education, new insights can replace those that become impracticable or redundant, even when the established attitudes are highly emotionalized and dependent. Overdependence on the comfort of old authorities, despite the fact that new situations call for a reexamination of old authoritarian attitudes, is one of the chief disadvantages of authority as a way of knowledge.

Often ignored in a consideration of authoritative knowledge is the claim of the Judeo-Christian heritage, and especially of the Christian church, to revealed knowledge. The claim is that God specifically and "in many and various ways" did inspire certain men to record his revelation in the form of a Bible (*ta bibla,* the books), which is in itself divine truth and as such is both the object and the guarantee of knowledge. The Bible is unique in that it is self-authenticated: "It says in the Bible again and again that the Word of God is being reported . . . [and] for centuries people have accepted it as such."[12] Also, while human writing and interpretation are involved in its presentation and preservation, the Bible is considered to be supernatural in origin and thus beyond the credibility tests normally required for proof or disproof. As religious leaders say, the Bible is accepted as the Word of God by faith and whenever possible by reason, but more often by personal religious experience (direct knowledge of God).

One of the present positions can well be called supernaturalism *in extremis,* not only holding to the concept of revelation but also insisting that each event of revelation is unique and miraculous. In this view God deals directly with the individual who then "knows" (God educates). T. F. Torrance well illustrates this position when he writes: "Christianity does not set out to answer man's questions. . . . [It] is above all the question the Truth puts to man at every point in his life, so that it teaches him to ask the right, the true questions . . . and to form on his lips the questions which the Truth by its own nature puts to him to ask of the Truth itself that it may disclose or reveal itself to him."[13]

The other extreme is a neonaturalism which is no longer concerned with the explanation of life and religion in terms of physical nature, but with the explication of divine revelation as a matter of human interrelationships in which God is known through the persons in human groups. The I-Thou relationship theory of Martin Buber is "gospel" for this extreme view—that in relationships and group fellowship we "know" (the group educates). Sara Little, in her book *Learning Together in the Christian Fellowship,* maintains that "Biblical scholars point out that a person's salvation comes to him, in part, as a member of a group." God seeks men, "confronting them in the midst of their experiences," leading men "to interpret their experiences in the light of their faith. Thus He reveals Himself. The creative interaction of men, struggling together to hear what God says in the events of today, becomes a medium by which He continues to confront them."[14]

Supernaturalism *in extremis* fails to establish a consistent epistemological position. On the one hand it seems to appeal to matters of fact, claiming that God is known through sensual experience divinely inspired on an individual basis, but on the other hand it establishes the usual conceptual-appraisal basis for religious language. Neonaturalism seems quite inoffensive, but on philosophical examination, the position though trivially helpful (group methods are helpful) is seen to be epistemologically barren. Groups are simply neither the source nor the grounds of knowledge, unless by the naturalistic fallacy of defining groups as knowledge, or relationships as knowing God. Paul L. Lehmann has proposed a compromise category which he calls a "faith-fact." "When Paul says that 'Jesus was seen,' he uses a very special word . . . not the word . . . in the ordinary sense of what we perceive with our eyes." He goes on to explain that this language deals with a special kind of "fact," which removes it from the category of contested knowledge.[15] Lehmann's proposal shows, I think, how imperative it is that more attention by the major theorists be given to epistemological decision in Christian education.

Modern Christian educators, consciously or unconsciously, hold to an epistemological position in which the categories of revelation are integral and determinative. All theorists hold that God is the source of truth and knowledge revealed (disclosed) in and through Jesus Christ, perhaps also through persons in community (especially the church), and in the unique self-communication, the Bible—the literature of revelation. Obviously, therefore, philosophical theologians must concern themselves with two great sets of questions: first, How can man know God? and How can he know that he knows God?; and second, What is revelation? and How is revelation known to be revelation?

D. M. Emmet has indicated the concern of many in her remark: "In order that philosophical criticism may be relevant and pertinent, it must raise the question of the criterion of revelation. What is the evidence on which theology claims to have to do with revelation? A criterion suggests some touchstone of judgment by which a revelation may be validated . . . or invalidated. And this suggests some principle of discrimination more ultimate in authority than the alleged revelation. It is this that the upholders of the latter deny. . . . If God speaks, it is not for us to judge or to criticize; we can only obey. A philosopher may be left asking how we know that God has spoken; if a particular religious tradition claims that He has done so, must we accept the claim at its face value?"[16]

The answer to Emmet's challenge divides Christian educators into two epistemological camps. The traditionalist answer reaffirms the orthodox self-disclosure of God and insists upon the unique and singular character of the revelation. The traditionalist is also a rationalist and tends to regard highly man's response to God with human reason guided only by the revelatory "given" character of the Bible and enlightened by theology. The other camp might be called the historical-experientialist, since its orientation is in terms of history and existentialism as opposed to metaphysics and rationalism. The advocates of this answer are also characterized by their interest in relationism, redemptivism, and presentism. J. V. L. Casserley declares he is in substantial agreement with Emil Brunner, who said: "It is characteristic of the biblical idea of revelation that it is not expressed in a unified formula . . ., an abstract idea. The biblical idea of revelation cannot be separated from the historical facts. . . . For this very reason an abstract definition of revelation is impossible."[17]

Of course, it may be that the two sets of questions posed

above concerning knowledge of God and its grounds, and revelation and its guarantee as knowledge, are not questions at all in the sense that we cannot "ask as a preliminary to any sort of problem-solving procedure . . . 'What kind of evidence would have a bearing on this question?' "[18] O'Connor further cautions against "the possibility of a very serious and dangerous kind of philosophical mistake, the . . . asking of questions that have the outward appearance of genuine . . . questions but which, on examination, do not satisfy [and he includes positive statements as well]—namely, possessing a possible range of evidence that, were it obtainable, would verify the statement or answer the question."[19]

The pro-Biblical camp is best represented by Smart, Wyckoff, Mayo Y. Smith, Boehlke, and R. R. Sundquist. Smart sets the pattern as he declares: "That God is the Creator and that the world and man are his creation is known, not by historical observation, but by faith, and the story of creation is a confession of that faith. It contains knowledge of God and man and the world that are basic to our entire Christian understanding of things. It is real knowledge, knowledge of the truth."[20] Wyckoff also argues, "If that to which . . . witness is given is the good news that God was in Christ reconciling the world to himself, then the referent is a real referent and the gospel is an actuality, an 'existent.' "[21] And in another place he suggests, "There is a prior gift, the ministry of the word."[22] Mayo Smith, in a working paper presented to the United Presbyterian Board of Christian Education, recommends, "The most that church education can do is to provide that knowledge from which a valid confession of faith may be made and to equip the man of faith to enquire into the nature of the Word and its demands, . . . to equip the church to fulfill its theological task."[23]

Boehlke comments that "knowledge [a concern to be learned] summarizes the basic data to be mastered . . . facts, . . . concepts, . . . [and] describes some of the necessary tools for discipleship. . . . The foundation of Christian nurture is rooted in the divine election . . . a series of mighty acts . . .

[and] God is known as a participating director of the drama of redemption. . . . Genuine knowledge is . . . the result of revelation."[24] and Sundquist adds: "The person who already has faith in God is the one who responds to him with faith. . . . God in the very act of coming to us provides the gift of faith so that we may know his presence. . . . He is known through faith, and he himself provides the faith by which he is known. . . . Yet faith wells up from our own experience of God, . . . and we always find that our faith is given to us by God, yet comes from our own experience."[25]

The pro-historical (experiential) camp is best represented by Cully, Miller, C. R. Stinnette, Sherrill, and Hunter. Cully commends the "existential approach, . . . grounded in the fact of the historical . . . action of God made known through the event of Jesus Christ. . . . Man's response to revelation may be called 'appropriation.' Since God is not an idea, and his revelation is not an abstract 'truth,' . . . the man of faith . . . is enabled to appropriate that which he knows to be . . . true."[26] Miller calls the historical-experience approach "the despair of philosophers" because the "Bible is not made up of abstract ideas" but "the interpretations of [concrete] events . . . [and] when the concrete language of the concrete story is made relevant in terms of . . . relationships, . . . they [intermediates] begin to discern the ways in which God is Lord of history."[27] Stinnette speaks with fervor of "the *passion* of knowledge [knowing and being united] . . . which is revealed in . . . personal encounter [and] is . . . profoundly revealing. . . . It is to know through a kind of prior knowledge . . . the truth as he participates in it. . . . It is felt and lived knowledge rather than logical thought, . . . a capacity to *make real* as well as a facility for facts!"[28]

Sherrill notes that "God is not merely suggested; he is disclosed . . . and visible to perception." The encounter "leads primarily not to knowledge *about* God but to knowledge *of* God, . . . the thorough knowledge that is derived from the experience of man," responding in the present.[29] Hunter also supports the notion of "presentism," noting that God continues to be active and present even *now* in our lives. "The Gospel which it is the privilege of Christian education and of every Christian to communicate, is the good news that the Triune God has acted, is acting now, and will continue to act in people's lives and throughout all His creation even while He waits and works for our response." Such knowledge of God, not only about God, issues in a living knowledge, and is "not truth concerning God but the living God Himself [words of William Temple]." "We are *engaging* with His presence and His activity."[30]

The writings of two "professional" theologians, Ferré and Georgia Harkness, in the field of religious knowledge reveal a similar epistemological decision to that of the historical-experiential group of Christian educators. Ferré supports the existentialist claim "that knowledge is more decisional than informational, . . . more created than discovered, more chosen than received. . . . Knowledge comes in the living, in the making, in the deciding. . . . Genuine knowledge must be concerned knowledge, related knowledge, applicable knowledge with meaning and direction in and for the actual experience of it. . . . Religion . . . deals with that which goes beyond ordinary experience and which therefore can illumine, transform, direct, and fulfill it. Somehow this more-than-the-ordinary reality can be known through the ordinary only from within it, existentially in experience, but yet can be known also reliably by true projection beyond it, in terms of a necessary choice of ultimates for which the constitutive religious event or experience . . . [is] the main gate to religious knowledge."[31]

Harkness announces that her quest for "Christian knowledge" will rest on objective grounds, but her objectivity seems to be founded on the concept of encounter. "Revelation [is] God's self-disclosure to the receptive spirit. . . . God does not disclose *truths*, . . . items of knowledge; rather, He imparts Himself . . . living presence, and from the transformation of life in this personal encounter convictions emerge." Further, her "historical realism" advocates, with Brunner, going "back behind the words of the Bible to the *facts* themselves," and she argues that the Holy Spirit may be understood "either theo-logically or experientially."[32]

To comment briefly on each of the twelve theorists is part of the built-in demand of a critique. Smart and Boehlke agree that "real" knowledge is revealed knowledge, to which Boehlke adds the extremist notion of "divine election." Wyckoff offers only circular support for religious statements: the referent is "real" and the gospel "actual" and "existential" because it is so declared by revelatory communication. Sundquist also suggests a propositional circularity—God provides faith so that faith can experience God and thus "know" him. Smith argues tellingly for limiting the objective of church education to the cognitive realm with one part of the task straightforward Bib-lical study. Cully and Miller set the grounds for knowledge in concrete events. For them, God and the Bible are not abstract ideas but "existential." Sherrill joins them in this, but notes a sensory ("visible") knowledge which is "thorough" and "pres-ent." Hunter supports Sherrill's "presentism" and also the notion that knowledge *of* and not *about* God is superior.

Stinnette underlines knowing with a psychological ground-ing as he speaks of "knowing and being united," and of feeling and living knowledge with a capacity to "make real." Ferré emulates Stinnette's existentialist posture, and his "decisional" knowledge "created," "chosen," and "living" seems to be a slogan system built upon his "choice of ultimates." However, his notion of knowledge from "actual" experience, yet from beyond it, and "more-than-the-ordinary reality known within it, in experience, and by projection beyond it," is vagueness at its worst. Harkness follows the "historical-experiential" line, and throughout her book the epistemological questions remain unanswered. For instance, How would one know an experience of/with/from the Holy Spirit except he be so informed con-ceptually? Thus, in the end, the experiential depends on the theological, and Ferré's observation is apt, that it is exceedingly important for Christian education to choose its theologians carefully.[33]

My purpose in this chapter is to stimulate an immediate and

wide-scale discussion on the relations between epistemology and Christian education. Such a happening is long overdue. Indeed, it is my belief that this apparent unwillingness of Christian educators to engage in a vindication of the epistemological validity of their discipline contributes to its innocuous status in the academic community. The natural epistemological category for Christian education is a matter of appraisal where statements are supported by a point of view (in this case, theological), except where facts are verified by observation or logic by a system of thought. The attempt to merge faith and fact by those who posit historical experimentalism or presentism cannot be considered epistemologically sound. And of course, the definition and demonstration of revelation remains a problem for traditionalism. However, since people continue to be concerned with religion as something important to their lives, theorists and theologians must face the epistemological issue honestly. To evade inquiry or declare an exemption is to reveal a triviality and to discourage an earnest search for truth. Matters of faith, like other appraisals, are always subject to a constant challenge for clarity as well as improved verification methods. Such is the quest to know.

PART TWO

Substantive Decisions
and Commitments

CHAPTER V

The Decision to "Meet Needs"

THE CONCEPT of "needs" and the attendant concept of "needs policy" in educational theory are without doubt two of the most influential concepts in the basic philosophical decisions of modern Christian education. The term "needs" has a common use as well as a narrower, more literal use. Reference to the dictionary reveals that "needs" has a descriptive meaning, especially when one discusses physical lacks or a state of deficiency or extreme wants; for instance, "Man needs water to preserve the necessary liquid content of the body." However, the most common use of "need" is mainly normative and prescriptive. Such usage carries with it the implication that certain criteria are diagnosed to be absent and also that the speaker or writer knows what the subject ought to be doing to make up the deficiency. The generalized "needs" statement tends to be guilty of the most common category mistake: the use of a word in the wrong logical category, in this case, confusing explanation and description with evaluation and prescription.

Christian education theorists rely very heavily on "needs" statements to justify the "needs policy" (curriculum should meet the "needs" of the student). Hunter, who, as director of the Episcopal Church's Department of Christian Education, issued a prepublication document to the Seabury Series entitled *The New Program of Christian Education*, which indicated their reliance on "needs" and "needs policy," asks, in Part II, "Where does it start?"

It starts in relation to a need. The new program now undergoing experimentation in more than thirty parishes has its origin at a point in people's experience where the Christian gospel always takes hold. This beginning is not necessarily made with reference to any need of the moment, for some needs are much more superficial than others. Indeed, there is only one need which really qualified—the need to feel the effects of being included within the redemptive fellowship of the Christian Church when the Church is really the Church.

Every living person at every age level is in need of redemption. By this we mean that he is in need of being saved from himself, from a self which apart from God is the inescapable victim of selfishness. This is true of infant, child, and adult. It is the universal condition of mankind, and there is only one remedy for it. . . . Only God who made us to be members of His family can restore us. This He wants to do through His Church.

The need to be saved from oneself gains expression at every age level, and as it does so the Church's work is being laid out for it. . . . In the areas of need where children and adults are revealing their own need for redemption, each in his own way, is to be found the place where the Gospel is relevant now. Such a wall of separation has been built between a man's world and his Church that it is common for people to suppose that meeting . . . needs is the responsibility of parents while the Church's business is to teach the faith . . . but there is no separation between the two. Teaching the faith takes place when the faith is encountered and embraced as well as assimilated. The Church is the fountainhead of the only power capable of meeting these needs, and the Church loses this power if it is confined within the walls of a church building. A teaching program which would really teach must become a program which nurtures by relating a child's need to the answer and action which Almighty God has provided.

If we wish to identify this need at each age level we will be greatly helped if we look for some fairly obvious manifestation of acceptance or rejection. Each of [our] needs . . . is either a desire for acceptance or a reaction against rejection, or both; and each can be complicated by causing the person himself to set in motion attitudes of acceptance and rejection. The job of identifying these needs and deciding precisely which ones are uppermost at specific age levels is not a task which should be given to each parish and mission of our [Episcopal] Church. This is a job for the national department and it is the first operation which the national department [of the denomination] has performed in the development of each of the experimental curriculum units. . . . [The Seabury Series began] to appear in 1955.

In adolescence, for instance, there is a very prominent demonstration of a common encounter with acceptance and rejection in a young person's surging desire to be accepted by the . . . group in his school and community. It is doubtful whether any other desire runs as deeply and is as all-consuming during the junior high and senior high years. Even when boys and girls are accepted by the desirable social set of their class, then they live in secret or open fear that they will forfeit their right to belong and lose favor with the other class leaders.

Like all mankind, a junior high youngster needs acceptance. By himself, apart from his fellows and not wanted by them, he knows he is lost. And the tragedy of his situation is to be seen in the fact that he cannot receive the acceptance he really needs and unknowingly craves from any group of people which relies on its own resources to do the things which ought to be done. The kind of acceptance every person needs is the kind we must have when we least deserve it, and this cannot be supplied by the power of man alone. This is the love of God which is not known out of relationship with God. This is redemption at a junior high level and at every age level.

The Bible, the Prayer Book, the sacraments, and the faith of the Christian creeds have been given to man to feed the parish family in relation to just such needs as this deep need of a junior high [youth]. The relationship is to be established now. The feeding and nourishing take place now. The focal point of attention and the point of contact with our people is this continuing need to be included now in the redeeming community. Here is where the new program of Christian education starts.[1]

Hunter's promotional statement has been reproduced with only minor deletions in order to demonstrate the Seabury commitment to needs policy. His article illustrates the most frequent use of the concept of needs in education, to prescribe certain actions or programs, a use that usually results in the identification of the need and often a list of auxiliary needs. Hunter's prescription of the need ("the only one need which is really qualified"), to be included in the redemptive fellowship and thus to be saved from himself, is offered as an explanatory answer to a diagnosed deficiency. However, it actually provides information only to the extent that we know that Hunter believes people lack what he prescribes for them. Further, he indicates that Seabury will be interested in and will identify "areas of need where [people reveal] their own need for redemption." Hunter's formula for discovering needs is to look for manifestations of acceptance or rejection at each age level, a job that he says is not a task of the local parish but of the national department. The implicit appeal to psychological deficit states also seems to imply a motivational use of needs; however, at the foundation of the descriptive-appearing use is the underlying notion of prescriptions to match the objective assumed in the need.

Hunter also places the Seabury Series directly in the center of the needs policy stance. He argues that while the common supposition assigns parents the role of meeting needs, actually only the church has the "power capable of meeting these needs." Hunter urges that "a teaching program which would really teach" must "relate a child's need to the answer and action which Almighty God has provided." Here is introduced the educational program which B. Paul Komisar calls the "needs-curriculum."[2] In his excellent analysis of needs, needs-policy, and needs-curriculum, Komisar points out that "the general proposal that schools meet students' needs is trivial [meet requirements or directives!] or indeterminate [Which "needs" are to be met?] or unsupported [specific and individual goals], depending on what a need is taken [or stipulated] to be."[3] The Hunter statement obviously fits the third category.

Much of the modern emphasis of Christian education is on meeting needs. Sherrill, for example, asks two great questions of the Presbyterian Church in the United States (Southern). "How far is this branch of the . . . [church] meeting the needs that confront us. . . . And what should we do . . . through . . . religious education, to meet these needs more adequately?" And in another place he exhibits the natural confusion on need statements. "Definition of the nature of human need is a task for philosophical or theological thought; the analysis of need is a task for scientific method."[4] Similarly, S. Little proposes that "the church needs to provide people with a kind of fellowship in which they can feel that their needs are respected and in which the whole group seeks to help them with their needs."[5] Further, Kennedy reports on the development of the *Christian Faith and Life* curriculum of the United Presbyterian Church that the "content will be chosen and used according to the needs and interests of the growing person . . . [and] methodology . . . designed to teach the Gospel as the revelation of God to meet human need."[6]

Miller notes that the secret of Christian education lies in meeting four needs: (1) love and acceptance; (2) law and order (need of discipline); (3) freedom to grow; and (4) a sense of the mystery of God.[7] Stinnette argues that "the human being is an organism endowed with certain capacities and needs, . . . the need to adapt . . . [and] the need to find his ultimate identity and meaning."[8] Both are firmly in the "needs policy" group, recommending almost impossible tasks for Christian education. But the extreme assurance was given to the General Convention of the Episcopal Church as a Christian Education Department member promised that "with the revision of the Seabury Series . . . the National Council will have a church school program designed to meet the needs of the whole church."[9]

Some of the writers proposed specialized and highly metaphysical needs. A review of some of these follows: Boehlke, for one, remarks that "there is also learning within the context of need and of the insufficiency of meeting this need."[10] Howe, using the word "need" in the title to his book, *Man's Need and God's Action*, fully subscribes to the needs policy, but describes the "deepest want of all" in answer to his pseudo question "What does man really want?": "The desire *to be at one with someone, to have someone who can be at one with us, and through whom we can find at-oneness with all.*" He also notes that "the full truth about human love, therefore, is that it both meets and does not meet our needs; that is, the more we have, the more we want."[11] Obviously, the answer to our needs is God's love, reconciliation, and restoration.

Crawford asks "just how far the organization structure and program of their parish are effectively meeting the needs of the souls for whom they are responsible" (as if there were some way of answering his question). And in another place he urges the parish with homiletical fervor to meet "the child's need to become the sort of person God made him capable of becoming."[12] Wyckoff quotes a report of the Executive Conference of the Division of Educational and Medical Work of the Board of National Missions: "A Christian institution is called into existence by Christians in order to meet certain pressing needs. Its life span is only as long as those needs or other compelling emergent needs endure."[13]

The needs policy is so well-promoted by Christian education theorists that statements and assertions purporting to identify needs are put forward as authoritative generalizations, often with the use of an adjective almost always as ambiguous as the word "needs" itself. These will be listed in alphabetical order of the first letter of the adjective.

1. "actual needs"—The content of statements of objectives changed, from broad concepts derived from philosophy, to emphasis upon the actual needs . . . of individuals in a dynamic society. (L. C. Little)[14]
2. "affectional needs"—[The Lutheran pamphlet *The Functional Objectives for Christian Education* speaks of the second most important function of the family as] meeting affectional needs.[15]
3. "basic needs"—A child is understood to have certain basic needs. . . . This insight from psychology has become popular parlance. (Cully)[16]
4. "deepest needs"—Man's deepest needs . . . are his potential needs to become fully human within his full environment, natural, human, moral, and spiritual. (Ferré)[17]
5. "existential needs"—Part of the teaching process is the re-

evaluation of needs so that superficial "wants" are transformed into existential needs. (Grimes)[18]

6. "human needs"—The Church confronts the individual with God in whom inheres the gracious power to meet every human need. (*Objectives*)[19]

7. "individual and social needs"—Every element in the entire program of the church has religious education significance in meeting individual and social needs. (*Curriculum Guide*)[20]

8. "psychological need"—The filial impulse is the natural root of religion, and . . . the Christian experience of God as Father answers to this psychological need. (Yeaxlee)[21]

9. "real needs"—The goals of the individual are frequently reflected in his interests but are not necessarily commensurate with his real needs. (*Objectives*)[22]

10. "religious needs"—It is the religious needs of the group . . . which shall finally determine the activities, method, and materials of the curriculum of Christian education. (*Curriculum Guide*)[23]

11. "specific needs"—Theology is a pattern . . . that must . . . be *creatively adjusted* to each person in order to meet the person's specific needs. (Ferré)[24]

12. "spiritual need"—The spiritual need of man transcends all particular moral requirements. It is need for the renewal of life at the personal center through the healing power of grace. (D. D. Williams)[25]

13. "substantial need"—This is "education as need-meeting activity." . . . A need, educationally speaking, is that kind of valid and important concern, not a superficial but a substantial one. (Heim)[26]

14. "true needs"—As Christians we know that the true needs and problems of life can be seen only in the light of the Gospel. (*Basic Principles*)[27]

15. [And the *Leader's Guide of the Episcopal Church School Teacher's Workshop* (1954) asked:] What do children's individual needs have to do with the Gospel? Generally it is acknowledged that a child needs to belong—that he needs love, acceptance and discipline. . . . How may I, in my specific task, provide for some of the basic needs of children?

1. The need to belong—At what point do I reject anyone? Are there children I cannot love?
2. The need for achievement—Do I do everything my-
   self . . . or [permit] the children to try tasks and give
   them guidance for their own success?
3. The need for freedom from fear—How do I contribute to . . . anxiety? In what ways do I threaten
   their growth?
4. The need for love and affection—Am I honest in my
   love . . . or am I only sentimental in my approach to
   children?
5. The need for release and freedom from guilt—Do I
   give . . . understanding? Am I forgiving?
6. The need for knowledge and understanding—Do I
   recognize that which the child needs and wants to
   know?
7. The need for discipline—Do I instead see the child's
   need for punishment [rather than] Christian discipline?[28]

There seems to be little question that Christian education
theorists make use of the prescriptive sense of needs and needs
policy and build thereon a needs curriculum, a system or program of education of which "meeting needs" is a title. A
majority of the writers either prescribe their own or a well-
established metaphysical or theological term or set of terms to
justify the use of "need," the results of which have been described and illustrated above. All seem to advertise that there
is in fact an empirical scale on which "the need," along with
other but less important needs can be observed, and thus described in matter-of-fact statements. What they are saying is,
"Scientists have told us what the needs of students are. Therefore, do X (educational task) to meet these needs." What really
happens is that certain age-level characteristics as noted by
psychologists become, on translation, age-level needs standing
in some relation to *the need* presupposed in the basic theological commitment—man's sin and God's salvation. Hunter is
getting at this in his book *Christian Education as Engagement,*
where defining "need" as man's religious situation (the need

of redemption by God), he concludes: "This is the situation of need for which Christian education exists."[29]

The main arguments of this chapter are thus seen to be twofold: first, that though need statements may be scientifically grounded in certain instances, the decision to teach to meet needs is actually a value judgment and not the scientific decision that Christian education theorists indicate; and second, that need statements are themselves prescriptive and not descriptive. Roughly speaking, certain needs—for instance, the need for food and water, which to lack would be injurious to a person as an individual—can be talked about, explained, and resolved on scientific grounds. However, the attempt to adapt education to needs—for instance, "the need to feel the effects of being included within the redemptive fellowship of the Christian Church"—illustrates the conceptual confusion of making normative recommendations based on socially approved or institutionally determined goals, even though they sound like explanation of fact based upon scientific investigation.

The intent of this critique, therefore, is to show that at the commonsense level, "need" is a normative term which prescribes a set of goals to match the diagnosis of "what ought to be" with "what is." "Meeting needs" with educational programs is thus concluded to be prescriptive and not descriptive. As Edward Farley has pointed out, while the teacher may elicit from his students their "real needs," it is obvious that he knows when they fail to report these needs, "apparently because the teacher already knows their Real Needs."[30]

CHAPTER VI

The Decision
to Emphasize "Experience"

M ODERN Christian educators are committed in the debate between content-centered curricula and experience-centered curricula strongly on the side of experience. John Heuss boasted that the Episcopal Seabury Series helped "to change religious learning from verbal repetition to living experience."[1] Whether or not his boast is accurate, "experience" is a term in need of definition. The dictionary gives several senses in which the term is used. One sense names experience a "trial, proof, or test; the observation of a fact, or of events happening." Another dictionary sense notes that experience is "the knowledge gained from living or from the changes or trials of life." In philosophy it is taken to be the "knowledge acquired through perception [by the senses]." In religion it is said to be the "feeling connected with conversion [or like events]." A dictionary sidenote suggests that experience may be an individual reaction to what one lives through or an activity which trains or teaches. Experiential is said to mean "empirical, based on experiment and observation." There is another sense in which experience is used—vicarious experience. While the two words are antonyms, nevertheless it is obvious that some experiences possible to adherents of a religious faith must of necessity be vicarious—as they "experience" religious phenomena through personal mystical activity or mental (or psychological) participation in another's experience.

The term sells itself readily to those looking for a scientific-sounding organizing principle in education; however, the obvious empirical context seems to fall away and analysis of how it is used and in what context must be provided. Taking

the Seabury commitment on the side of experience literally,
W. S. Lea asked in his *Episcopal Churchnews* editorial, "Is
the central theme of the Christian revelation really compatible
with an 'experience-centered' technique?"[2] However, *Christian
Education: Guide I,* explained the Seabury commitment to
experience on the ground that "experience is the best teacher."
Noting the recognition of this tendency in secular education,
the *Guide* urges that "a program of Christian education for
a parish will be a plan of guiding people into experiences in
the Christian pattern of life, . . . a plan which will select these
experiences for different individuals and age groups which
will best enlist the active interest and vigor of those participating. . . . It will not be a plan that will merely inform people
about the Christian Life. . . . Christian experience is the best
Christian educator."[3] There is incompleteness bordering on
circularity through this brief attempt to justify a methodological decision. Circularity is seen in the claim that experience
is educator, since people must be guided into experiences by a
plan that will be selective among experiences according to the
criteria of Christian values, rather than the initiative remaining
with experience.

Bridging Some Gaps quotes Vieth as saying: "In the broadest sense of the term all life is the curriculum. There is no
experience which does not have an influence on what people
become. [And in a more specific sense] . . . all those activities
and experiences which are initiated or utilized by the Church
for the achievement of the aims of Christian education."[4] Now
there may be a way of giving sense to the first sentence, but
you would have to drain all commonsense meaning out of
"curriculum." Further, to note the influence of experience on
people is not very profound. The difficulty with broad statements calling everything experience is that any statement
about learning only from experience becomes trivial. Still,
the attempt to limit the statement to the confines of a church
does not save the patent ambiguity. Charles Penniman and
Miller agreed in principle with Vieth on the experience curriculum. Penniman said, "It seems to me that there is a growing

realization that curriculum is not primarily a matter of writing; that it is a matter of planned and guided experience where people are."[5] Miller wrote: "The curriculum is the experience of the learner under guidance. . . . It involves every activity of the child from the moment he reaches the Church property until he leaves. . . . The entire life of the parish provides opportunity for Christian education, and in itself comprises the curriculum."[6]

Since Miller is a distinguished and influential professor of Christian education, it seems important to make a fuller critique of his contribution on the subject of experience. He holds that "the fundamental law of learning is *experience,* and second only to it is *repetition.*"[7] He talks of the "learner in a life process . . . [where the] method . . . is centered in the growth of the child rather than things to be learned."[8] Miller concludes: "A little child learns primarily through activity, and that what he sees or touches or smells is of greater significance than what he hears [by way of being told]. He can learn great lessons about God because he can see, touch, or smell a flower or a doll or a baby."[9] On the matter of experience as a "fundamental law of learning," Miller displays only his enthusiasm for a slogan system.

It is true, of course, that in a broad sense experience is one way of learning, yet undiscriminating use of the term can be either trivial (We learn by learning) or analytical, depending on a stipulative or persuasive definition of experience as meaning "that from which one learns." Actually, of course, both experience and learning need careful definition; otherwise, they will shift meaning and allow ambiguity to take over. Miller also must be asked to clarify how a learning or a teaching method can be "centered in the growth of a child," if he expects colleagues to take his proposals seriously, because to teach them means to teach them *something.* Further, regarding his comment that a child learns "a great lesson about God" because he perceives certain objects, Augustine would argue that he could not, for the reason that senses cannot yield knowledge of God. Miller seems to join most of the other Seabury theorists in suggesting the senses as a verifier of the suprasensual, immaterial God. It is self-contradictory, especially at the bar of public verification.

But Miller has another theory to support an experience curriculum. He says: "Life [experience]-centered teaching is sound psychologically, pedagogically, and philosophically. It is the natural and quickest way to learn." But he warns the method is no end in itself. A theology is needed. "The objectives, theory, and methods . . . need to be undergirded and perhaps altered by a more self-conscious theological reconstruction. . . . At the same time, there needs to be a facing of the problem of relating content to method in an organic whole."[10] Miller claims that "in theology properly interpreted lies the answer to most of the pressing educational problems of the day. The new element in educational theory is the discovery of the organic relation between doctrine and experience, between content and method, between truth and life." He also calls worship "the experience-centered method *par excellence* for educational purposes."[11]

Miller cautions, however: "This is not a plea to return to a content-centered curriculum [which regarded as an end in itself leads to verbalism and a "Christianized parrot"], [nor] . . . to indoctrination [which] . . . implies a kind of authority which is consistent with controlled propaganda rather than with the growth of individuals in the Christian way of life. . . . The center of the curriculum is a twofold relationship between God and the learner. The curriculum is both God-centered and experience-centered."[12] Notice that Miller now argues for the incorporation of a "new" methodological decision—a theological one. His extravagant claim that theology holds the answer to most contemporary educational problems should have been supported by naming one such problem. It may be that he had in mind his "organic relation" concept as a cure-all elixir, but it is not a cure for any one educational ill. Even worship, claimed by Miller to be "the experience-centered method *par excellence* for educational purposes," seems to be an experience in a sense nonpublic and nonverifiable except to those who acknowledge the mystical and personal sense which the in-group intend in their use of the word. His final claim to both a God-centered and an experience-centered curriculum appears to be another unsupported enthusiasm almost meaningless except in a context where the word "experience" is stipulatively ambiguous.

The International Curriculum Guide: Book One notes that "Christian education concerns itself with the experience of growing persons . . . [but] it is the object . . . to introduce control into experience in the direction of Christian ends, . . . to touch as large an area as possible of the experience of the learner and lift it to the Christian level." The report speaks of revealing "significant experiences" for each age group and recommends "units of guided experience," which are introduced as experience, and Christian educational objectives are matched and related. The document presents a classification of numerous activities and relations on the assumption "that there is religious meaning and value in every normal and significant human experience."[13] Of course, the words are all here that might clarify an emphasis in Christian education on experience, but its effectiveness is lost in the circularity of argument which fails to resolve the dilemma of the primacy of individual experience and the necessity to have experience quantitatively explained or qualitatively assured by the church.

Wyckoff takes up a companion theme as he relates the experience decision to curriculum-building based on "certain Christian ideas and certain generalizations about experience." He says, "The content must tap the real experiences of the pupil," and yet he adds, "The curriculum tells us what experiences are necessary," and that methodology "answers the question of how these experiences shall be introduced into the life of the pupil." Indeed, "the transmission of the Christian faith . . . is primarily a matter of the re-creation of human experience into experience that is divinely redeemed." And, "Christian personality develops as our experience is reconstructed, transformed, and redeemed by God in Christ . . . [which is] the refinement [and organization] of experience with . . . Christian

standards."[14] Wyckoff tries to give life to the notion of personal
experience as it is informed or transformed by the prescriptions
and guidance of a religious category of experience. However,
if all he means is the injection of religious notions into life
situations, his attempt is trivial. Or, if he means simply that a
church identifies "real" or otherwise qualitative experiences
as those which a person ought to have, he offers nothing
educationally helpful.

Sherrill uses the word "encounter" as a synonym for "experience," arguing that "it leads primarily not to information as
such, but to the actual experience of the Person and the events
with which the information deals." He speaks of the "perception of the themes . . . in the Bible" and explains that "what a
particular revelatory event utters is 'a word from the Lord' to
those who are able to perceive it. . . . The encounter thus is
described as an experience of seeing, hearing, entering into
dialogue," but more than merely "seeing" and "hearing," to
perceive revelatory events thus is to perceive "in faith . . . that
which is 'unseen' by the ordinary operation of the mind . . .
characterized by . . . great clarity of perception."[15] Since
Sherrill makes so much of the "principle of perception," it calls
for specific comment at this point. In ordinary use "perception"
remains very close to its primary connotation of "that which
can be apprehended by the senses." However, a peripheral
meaning which includes insight or intuition softens the meaning and encourages Sherrill's speculations on "experience" in
Christian education. Unfortunately, the contradictory usages
cannot be held in the same claim. Either we take "experience"
to mean sensory perception or we must admit that we are
using another category where experience is highly conceptual,
vicarious, or at best a faith commitment. In the above argument
it is obvious that Sherrill holds the latter notion of perception,
but still wants to gain the obvious values of the ordinary use of
the word.

He illustrates the principle of perception by noting that
"Biblical material is a means for changing the perception of the
meaning . . . expressed in symbolical terms such as hearing a

voice which gives a command, seeing a vision, . . . [or] comparable experiences . . . [which] have accompanied profound changes in the meaning of life."[16] Sherrill here is guilty of a conceptual confusion between "perceive" and "conceive" and their related epistemological decisions. Objects are perceived and statements about observation are called matter-of-fact. Definitions are conceived and statements about the relation of ideas are called matter-of-logic. The switching back and forth must be dimly viewed by the philosopher. Howe also uses the word "encounter" calling "experience in relationship" primary in Christian education, and the transmission of the subject matter of the historical faith secondary. "The content of our faith was born of God's action and man's response—a divine-human encounter. It is possible, however, to reduce it to subject matter and substitute the transmission of subject matter for the encounter [experience], with the assumption that it will accomplish the same purpose (although it cannot, it never has, and it never will)."[17] Of course, Howe points out, as we might expect, that "encounter-experience" as a phenomenon cannot be reduced to subject matter and transmitted, but must be experienced. Just how it is to be experienced is never explained.

Williams attempts to explain the Tillichian "method of correlation" as resolution of the concrete experience of people as it is confronted in encounter with the Christian gospel. Williams seems to follow Tillich in recommending that Christian education will profit from an application of the method. On one pole of correlatives is the human situation—the ontological anxiety of human experiences, death, guilt, meaninglessness. On the other pole is the gospel message which speaks to human experiences—the disclosure of God as being-itself, life, redemption, and meaning. Williams points to the task of Christian education, therefore, as "drawing out from the person his questions . . . [from] the center of his being" and addressing "the message of the Christian faith . . . to the person . . . [as] the answers . . . are given [revealed]."[18] However, while enthusiasm for Tillich's method is easy to arouse, on careful analysis of the method, the enthusiasm is just as easily deflated. The human situation is categorized as experiential by Tillich and as such should be available to scientific investigation. But the symptoms noted are all metaphysical and therefore depend ultimately on a point of view or on the prescription of the one who notes the symptoms, e.g., guilt and meaninglessness. So in the end, the method is shown to be completely prescriptive, competing with other religious prescriptions. To be sure, Tillich himself argued, "We are asking: How do we make the message heard and seen and then either rejected or accepted? The question *cannot* be: How do we communicate the Gospel so that others will accept it? For this there is no method."[19]

Cully speaks of "the existential depth of a child's experience" and argues that children understand "on a completely human plane . . . [by] another basic experience . . . [that] the gospel is God's answer to man's need." Further, she predicts that "there comes a moment in a life when God is no longer simply a word or an idea but a living reality whom the person recognizes." Actually, she does admit to "the inadequacy of the popular understanding of 'experience,'" opting for the substitution of the word "existential." The substitution will matter little, for the substantive decision remains. Does Cully mean that a child "experiences" sin, guilt, and death and God's responses to these theological notions? Further, does she mean that a child "recognizes" God in the ordinary sense, or is she retreating to the notion mentioned earlier of seeing "with eyes of faith."[20]

Hunter, concerned with Christians having "a real experience with God now," proposes that "an engagement methodology . . . [or] religious issues . . . [be] selected as the organizing principle" for Christian education. "When religious issues are selected . . . a search begins for the particular manifestations of a given religious issue . . . common at a given age or experience level." He defines "religious issue" as "any issue which is the consequence of engagement."[21] The words may be somewhat different—Hunter uses engagement as a synonym for encounter or experience—but the implication is no more adequately sustained. Indeed, the notion that a scientifically established set of religious issues is empirically obtainable drawn from experience and common to a given age level is unverifiable.

To sum up, Christian education theorists try to use the notion of experience in at least three different ways. First, they use it as a slogan to add weight to a corrective of the less imaginative and often-times boring methods of traditional education. As such, emphasis on the skeptical attitude, the process of inquiry, and the methods of observation and experiment encouraged along with the presentation of information is to be highly commended.

Second, however, they use experience as a title for a motivational truism which points out that it is difficult to teach anyone anything unless it appeals to existing interests or unless the necessary interest can be created. This chapter has criticized this attempt because of its fundamental ambiguity and for its latent circularity; for instance, the notion that the experience of individuals is primary, but that experience is given meaning by and in the group.

Third, Christian educators use experience in a way that suggests ongoing observation and experiment, but in reality they switch to either "religious experience," a term descriptive of mystical, psychological, or vicarious experience, or to a more trivial concept of the injection of religious notions into life situations. Their use of experience is thus shown to be matter-of-logic, analytical (true by definition) language, meaning at the most "create interests," and prescribing a specific educational program to bring this about, and not matter-of-fact or descriptive language at all.

CHAPTER VII

The Commitment
to "Relationship Theology"

PROBABLY the most firm and influential commitment of many modern Christian education theorists is made to a fully developed concept from existentialism known as "relationship theology." It is obvious that this key concept is deeply philosophically laden, carrying with it a prior theological commitment. Yet the word "relationship" can be used in a philosophically neutral context and in that use does not require analysis. The dictionary shows that the word "relate" means "to ally by connection or kindred; connection perceived or imagined between things; a certain position occupied by one thing with regard to another." "Relation" means "the state of being related," and "relations" means "the connections between or among persons or things." There is a use of relationship in logic, where categorical statements are called *relational* statements and are classified according to symmetry (relation is reversible) and transitivity (relation is not reversible). Using the rules of logic, one can describe almost all relations; for instance, if A is in relation to B, and if B is in relation to C, then A is in relation to C. A later argument will afford opportunity to apply this rule of relationship.

The commitment to a religious existentialist posture makes it necessary for us to examine the school of philosophy labeled existentialism. Of course, many existentialists argue that there is no school, but there is an existentialist metaphysical world view and a profound existentialist relationalism with a number of common elements, especially among the religious existentialists—Kierkegaard, Buber, Tillich, and Niebuhr (to name four who wielded noticeable influence upon Christian educators).

The influence stems not only from the ideas but also from the missionary zeal evidenced on behalf of the doctrine of relationship, following Kierkegaard's exhortation, "It is the God-relationship that makes a man a man."[1] Buber, in his lyrical and poetic *I and Thou,* assesses the meaning of the individual's life to be in the I-Thou relations which he can enter into with men and with God. "If I face a human being as my *Thou,* and say the primary word *I-Thou* to him, he is not a thing among things, and does not consist of things . . . to be experienced and described. . . . He is Thou and fills the heavens. . . . All else lives in *his* light. . . . When *Thou* is spoken, the speaker . . . takes his stand in relation. . . . All real living is meeting."[2] Also Buber insists, "A person makes his appearance by entering into relation with other persons."[3]

The common elements of religious existentialism adopted by many theorists are existence; freedom; the desperate predicament of man; the inability of man to help himself; the action of God to provide help through a Person (Jesus Christ) and persons to restore man to relationship with God, with others, and, some add, with himself. So obvious was the influence of existentialism on the Episcopal Seabury Series that C. E. Nelson entitled his review of the series for the *Union Seminary Quarterly Review* "Existential Christian Education."

Numerous authors, in line with existentialist posture, also raise and discuss the "great ultimate questions" of man noted variously as: "Who is God?" "Who am I?" "Who are you?" "How did we get here?" and "Where are we going?" Crawford puts the same questions in other words: "What are we here for?" "Is there any purpose in living?" and adds, "Without a satisfactory answer . . . life cannot begin to make sense."[4] Of course, the theorists have a predetermined metaphysical answer—the experiences of faith (the faith community), the need for acceptance (to be accepted for what I am), and love (even when I am unlovable).

One of the early Episcopal Parent's Manuals, *Apostles in the Home,* gives the prescribed answer. "It is exactly to questions like these that the Christian Gospel provides answers. The answers are never *abstract* but always related to actual experiences and life situations [we're all children of God.]"[5] The manual then gives a Kierkegaard parable, "The Divine Incognito," as explanation, which to some readers is very *abstract*, indeed. Actually, as O'Connor has pointed out,[6] the so-called existential questions are on closer scrutiny seen to be pseudo questions asked by those who wish to justify a particular philosophical-theological system, or to impress laymen with a verbal profundity.

On the subject of relationship theology Chaplin quotes Abbé Marc Oraison:

This is not an intellectual choice, nor a philosophical conviction, but the consent to a relationship with a living person . . . and each one of us enters into relationship with Him. . . . Religious education cannot be conceived of except in this way. . . . [It] consists in encouraging the child to enter into a personal and living relationship with Someone . . . [who], in this dialogue which he seeks in the very heart of man, has His word to say.[7]

Design for Methodist Curriculum continues the thought: "God comes to man, calling man into relationship with him. . . . As man responds to God in faith, love, commitment, and obedience, he finds that light is thrown on all his relationships and that he is empowered and enriched within these relationships."[8] Yeaxlee explains the phenomenon: "Life is organized and disciplined, finds meaning and direction, in active relationships between persons, and religion is the supreme form of such a relationship. . . . [It] is thus seen to be fulness of life, . . . a dynamic harmony."[9] And Ernsberger notes its influence, "The things that are taught, the meanings that are communicated, are conditioned to a great extent by the quality of the personal relationships that exist within the fellowship of the church [and] . . . through the quality of the . . . interactions."[10]

The case for relationship theology was probably first presented in Christian education theory by Sherrill. He defined relationship as "that which exists *between* two entities and affects them both, when they are brought to bear upon each other. . . . They 'do something to' each other. . . . The *process* of affecting each other . . . is interaction." Indeed, he argues that "*the self is formed in its relationships with others. . . .* Then it can begin from within to become what as yet it is not but might be." He points out that religious thought approaches the concept of relationship from the point of view of depth psychology while admitting that "in religious thought, 'relationships' are conceived in a cosmic frame of reference." Yet, he does mean relationships "to God, to other men, to oneself," a curious mixture of categories involving the word "relationship."[11]

Sherrill's definition seems quite inoffensive and not too far removed from the ordinary use. However, he immediately moves beyond it into the speculation that "self is formed in relationships." Now while this may someday be established as scientific fact, it is not universally so regarded at the moment and therefore exposes Sherrill's move as normative and not descriptive. His goal of self becoming "what as yet it is not but might be" is enthusiastic prescription, for he has a program to bring it off—the gift of power, which admittedly is cosmic in its frame of reference. However, his trinity of relations— God, others, and self—just do not pack into the same reference of language. Indeed, relationship with God can be conceived, relations with man may be perceived, but no language, logic, or experience will sustain the strange notion of relationship of self to self.

Miller was also among the first Christian educators to develop rather fully as the "clue" to Christian education "a two-fold relationship between God and the learner . . . in the fellowship of the Church," also "the right relationship with God and his fellows." Granted a prior metaphysical premise, these statements are not too difficult to accept, but Miller presses on: "The human integration of a child does not evolve from his *idea* of his parents. It comes from his *relationship* with his parents. So also, his religious integration does not come primarily from *his idea of God.* It comes from his *personal relationship* with God."[12] Unfortunately, the words "integration" and "relationship" need analysis before this statement can be given any serious consideration.

Miller has much to say about "integration" (of the Christian personality). He calls it "the goal of religious instruction," unachievable in character education (ideals alone), indoctrination (beliefs alone), or in social adjustment. It must be "deeper integration . . . which results from a deep and abiding personal relationship between God and man. It flows from a right religious adjustment which is a basic process of living." Later Miller says that "Christian growth is a process of increased integration centered on the living God who is in our midst."[13] In another place, he concludes that "a sound 'relationship theology' is the only protection the teacher has" to questions children ask, for example, "Why did Jesus die?"[14]

Miller's introduction of the concept of integration is little help in the quest for the meaning of relationship. As a matter of fact, since integration seems to mean "being in the right relationship with God," integration can hardly be offered as a definer of relationship. Further, Miller with Sherrill offers only the notion that the understandable relationship between living persons can be transferred to an understanding of the relationship of a person with God. Obviously, he can only bring this off in extraordinary language, such as the ceremonial and analogical language used in worship or prayer. The difficulty is that Miller uses the ordinary notion of relationship from which he shifts to a theological notion unsupported except for analogical and Biblical language. And his commendation of relationship theology as a tool to solve or escape dilemmas of human experience has nothing from logic or life to support it.

Howe's commitment to relationship theology is seen in the advice that relationship is as essential to a child as his food, and represents his primary need. He admits to the influences of both Tillich and Buber in his existentialist stance. "Our loneliness, then, is in part a result of the nature of existence, because existence itself means the separation of person from person. . . . Dr. Paul Tillich points out that this state of separation is a state of sin. . . . All our life, therefore, is an effort to overcome our separation and to find each other in fulfilling relationship." Later he notes that "the deepest significance of religion has to do with our attempt . . . to mend the break between ourselves [others] and our God. . . . We want to be 'at one' with Him Who is the 'ground of our being.' "[15]

Howe makes a strong plea for what he and others call the "language of relationship" in teaching ("I need the grace to *be* in order to help [you] . . . to *become*,") and for "a ministry of relationship." "We may experience [God's] . . . love through person-to-person encounter with those who are born into the [love] relationship . . . not by reading about it." Howe calls on Buber for support in his account of relationship theology, as he gives Buber's I-Thou concept full theological meaning: "The word I . . . and the word God (for which we can substitute the word "Thou" because it refers to God and our neighbor as well)." Later, Howe substitutes the words "Eternal Thou" for God and notes that man's use of the I-Thou meanings "will help him choose to be in relation to God and others in spite of the [other] meanings in him that will drive him to choose against man and God."[16]

A fuller discussion of Howe's unique notion of teaching will be found in Chapter IX. It is important to this chapter to note Howe's supreme dependency on relationalism. His use of the word "experience" to discuss the love relationship, for example, is misleading, and meaning is supplied only by theological definition and presupposition.

Harvey Cox, in his critique of modern Christianity, *The Secular City*, speaks of a misunderstanding of Buber which Howe and others seem to have accepted uncritically. Cox comments that it is hard to believe that Buber meant his categories I-Thou and I-It to be exclusive of all other relationships, or that all our relationships would (or indeed, should) be of the deep, rich, and rare variety of the I-Thou type. Of course, Buber did not offer a further discrimination of other types of relationships short of the I-It category in which the person is reduced to the status of an object. Cox calls this an unnecessary dichotomy, and suggests an I-You relationship which would be of the public type, responsible "neighborliness," but not sentimental "togetherness."[17]

Howe's use of Buber's I-Thou concept does little to explicate the justification of educational method. Rather, Howe's extensive use of Buber evokes the comment that the educational application of the I-Thou concept is either so pious that it is incomprehensible, or else it is so trivial that it is not worthy of serious philosophical consideration. Howe later changes the relational term to "relationship of acceptance" and labels it the appropriate method of church teaching since it "partakes of the very nature of the Church." Here Howe confuses categories. A practical choice of a teaching method is one thing, but the theoretical nature of an institution is quite another thing.

S. Little, supporting Howe on the language of relationship as well as the whole gamut of relationship theology notions, writes: *"The whole history of God's dealing with man is a record of His working with the individual in community. . . .* Biblical scholars point out that a person's salvation comes to him, in part, as a member of a group. . . . The creative interaction of men, struggling together to hear what God says in the events of today, becomes a medium by which He continues to confront them."[18] Grimes also takes up the apologia with the statement that "the human self emerges . . . from . . . human relationships [the family and the church, as] the 'I' of the child [is] confronted by the 'thou's' in his communities. . . . However, . . . fellowship on a Christian level is something which is given . . . yet . . . which does not become operative until man meets certain conditions, e.g., communion. [It is] . . . not primarily a human fellowship, [but] drawn from a divine source."[19] Smart joins in the necessary lip service to the notion of "a two-way relationship—with God and our fellow man," arguing with impeccable orthodoxy that "each relationship is dependent on the other." However, he later notes that our point of contact with God is our knowledge that beneath it all we are children of God, and that, however broken our relationship with God may be, we cannot break God's relationship with us.[20]

Little evidences her enthusiasm and little else in the assumptions that seek to explicate the "whole history of God's dealing" as "in community," and that "fellowship" is saving (redemptive). But her assessment that "the creative interaction of men" is the medium of divine-human confrontation is little more than her statement of preference and a prescription for "real" group life. Grimes, in his attempt to make Buber's relationalism meaningful, engages in what John R. Fry diagnosed as "instant Christian education," adding the Thou dimension.[21] And his confusing notion of fellowship as not only given, but also within the realm of meeting certain conditions is neither philosophically nor practically helpful. Smart, partaking of the obscure Biblicism of his heritage and theological alignment, notes a contradictory and strange use of relationship—it can be broken one way only. Obviously, this use is extraordinary.

Crawford seems to echo Howe, but with a different emphasis, namely, on the mechanics of a parish. "How far a parish is truly a parish depends on the common faith relationship [communicated through being in a faith community, the Fellowship] . . . together with their individual and collective commitment to the demands of this relationship as reflected in what goes on in the life of the Parish." If Crawford's prescription of what a parish ought to be could be made clear, it would always be possible to say, "Oh, that's not truly a parish!" Crawford quotes J. H. Oldham: "'We are persons only in relation with other persons.' This means that life finds its fulfillment only in community . . . [the ultimate purpose of life], a living response to the . . . 'Thou' of the universe [whom we meet] in the 'thou' of each personal encounter."[22] Certainly someone might ask, "What are we during the moments we are not in relationship or community?"

Crawford also echoes Sherrill as he remarks that "there is a threefold relationship that marks our existence as spiritual beings—relationship with God, with others, and with self. These . . . always go together. . . . Any one . . . points to the existence of the other two . . . [and] derives its meaning from its relation to the others."[23] The last argument contains some language and logical difficulties. It seems quite strange to speak of "our *existence* as spiritual beings." Indeed, it is also somewhat strange to link existence and meaning to relationships, inferring that relationship is prior to existence and meaning. The confusing logical move is seen to be a triadic relationship in which self is A, other B, and God C. What Crawford is saying is that A is in relation to B *only* if he is in relation to C; or that A is in relation to C *only* if he is in relation to B. This puts severe limitations on relationship. Actually, all that is being said is rather, "These relationships ought to obtain," which is either a moral claim or a prescription.

Hunter uses the term "engagement," but it still spells out relationship theology! His definition of engagement is the clue: "meeting, knowing (not knowing *about*), responding to or ignoring, loving, hating, . . . the experience we are having or ought to be having as Christians: namely, our changing and unchanging encounter with God, our response to His action, . . . the moment when God acts in or upon the life of an individual and the individual faces the obligation to respond. . . . For engagement is relationship, the ongoing experience of God knowing man and man knowing God and not knowing God, of man knowing man and not knowing man."[24]

It can hardly be denied that such a word as engagement has a function in religious language because it names a happening recognized quite widely as a religious experience. However, reduced to language where public acceptance and verifiability hold sway, the word "engagement" means "to meet or to involve." The move from human meeting to the human-divine encounter must be made in the context of religious language alone; therefore, no verifiability must be transferred from the public domain. However, Hunter poses another language problem when he speaks of a "changing *and* unchanging encounter." And only Hunter can reveal what he means by "knowing and not knowing" God and man!

Several other theorists testify to the educational significance of relationship theology. Cully says that the church teaches through relationships as "God's action takes place in and through the fellowship . . . seen through human relationships within the church."[25] Ferré notes that "the aim of Christian education is to help people gain a right relationship to God and to all men. . . . The truth and knowledge of Christian teaching, however, are those of human beings in the ultimate dimension of their togetherness."[26] And Boehlke offers the promise that "as learners in the church perceive relationships between themselves and the whole field of relationships, including God, dependable knowledge is gained. . . . [And] the nature of the relationship determines the depth of learning."[27] In view of the earlier analyses of similar notions, Cully, Ferré, and Boehlke are saying very little to assure our sanguine acceptance of their enthusiastic prescriptions. Indeed, their words are illustrative of the ambiguities and language shifts which are responsible for some of the flaws and omissions in the philosophical foundations of Christian education because of the commitment to relationship theology.

Our critique has established, first, that the shift from the philosophically neutral usage of the term "relationship" as a connection between things or persons to a religious existentialist commitment to the philosophical usage is a transmogrification of a serious nature. The move from the descriptive, ordinary notion of human, observable relations of living persons to the theological notion carrying a claim to similar, living relations, but based on analogy and Biblical language alone, calls for fuller inquiry and more adequate support.

Second, that while there is a lot to say for Howe's emphasis on the "language of relationships" as a factor in the educational process, yet without the "language of words" there would be little meaning coming from (out of) the feelings and responses of "experiences in relationship." Indeed, without words and ideas, there can be no adequate explanation.

Third, we noticed (following Harvey Cox) a puzzling omission of other common relationships in the Buber categories of I-Thou and I-It, an omission which makes the use of the notion as a recommendation for educational policy highly questionable. Further, it seems that religious educators use the Thou category in such a mystical way that its only service is to commend the sort of relationships that ought to exist in the church and in Christian education and not to describe the relations observed to be in fact existing.

The author of the Episcopal *Church School Teacher's Workshop* has supplied a fitting, one-sentence conclusion to this chapter's critique: "It seems to me there is something very profound about persons becoming persons in relationship to other persons."[28]

CHAPTER VIII

The Commitment to "Redemptive Fellowship"

R EDEMPTIVE" is a term widely used in Christian education materials, a fact which, on the surface, would not call for the attention of a philosophical critique. Surely this word has lost much of whatever neutral sense it once possessed, and is mostly a theologically laden term. Of course, one does talk of redeeming coupons, and the Bible does talk of "redeeming the time." However, the word "redemptive" has been relegated almost exclusively to theology, where, in spite of some controversy on the means of redemption, the theological meaning is rather clear, especially in theistic circles. In Christian education literature the common use is, of course, maintained. But some theorists seem to emphasize a special function of the term in making it a prescriptive adjective carrying evaluative overtones set in tune with overall normative objectives and commitments, moving the function from theological explanation to prescriptive educational policy. More on that later! First, a check of the basic definitions seems necessary.

The word "redeem" comes from the Latin *redimere*, which means "to buy back, ransom, or repurchase." In English usage it also means "to rescue, or liberate; to deliver, or save; to make amends for, to atone for, or to compensate." The theological usage is given as "to effect the ransom from sin and its penalty." Thus redeemer is "one who redeems or ransoms," specifically "Jesus Christ the Savior of the world." And redemption is "the act of redeeming, and [in theology] the purchase of God's favor by the death and sufferings of Christ, the ransom or deliverance of sinners from the bonds of sin and the penalties of God's violated law." Finally, the word "redemptive" means "redeeming or serving to redeem; relating to redemption." The Judeo-Christian Bible contains many references to redemption. The word is used of money payments for the recovery of property (Lev. 25:25), the firstborn (Num. 3:44–51), and the release of persons from slavery (Ex. 21:7–8). The idea of deliverance, especially by God, appears in Deut. 7:8 and Isa. 62:12 and 63:4. God as redeemer and the idea of redemption from sin occurs in Ps. 130:8, Isa. 41:14, and Job 19:25. Of course, the New Testament points to Christ as the Redeemer and, maintaining the Old Testament figure of "buying back" with Christ's sacrificial death as a ransom, also indicates that redemption from sin is a gift of God to match man's repentance and faith.[1]

Obviously, in the religious context and with the presuppositions of orthodox Christian theology, the word "redemptive" can be used meaningfully when it describes the activity of God in Christ and in the Spirit-filled church for the purpose of redeeming in the specific manner defined above. Therefore, Hunter is quite within the correct usage as he calls attention to "the redemptive activity of God in the Church through the Holy Spirit."[2] Wyckoff also qualifies with his prescription that "the church is the human instrumentality brought into being by God in Christ to continue his ministry of redemption to the world . . . [and] as the fellowship of the redeemed" functions to nurture and train.[3]

Before proceeding to an analysis of the questionable uses of the word "redemptive," some mention must be made of the modern commitment to the redemptionist school of theological thought which is distinguished from the creationist school. The redemptionist type of theology is generally committed to existentialist philosophy and tends to specialize in the study and interpretation of the data of theologically described experience, among which are "man's experience of being a sinner," powerless to save himself or to surmount the crisis of his own existence and "the way in which God in and through Jesus Christ has come to man's rescue and done that for him which he cannot do for himself."[4] The doctrines of atonement, redemption, or salvation make up a theme that is used to answer all other theological problems.

This type of theology has certain advantages. It keeps close to the somewhat more psychological-empirical area of religious experience. And it does present a singular, systematic, and simplified message and point of departure. Of course, the redemptionist emphasis has some disadvantages as well. It is simply too limited in its scope and it ignores too many areas of human life and experience. Casserley questions whether the so-called "point of departure" is genuine. "Can man really explain what he means when he declares himself to be a sinner without some reference to a doctrine of creation . . . in the light of which he is able to perceive that he is in fact a sinner?"[5]

Another quite different type of theology is the creationist theology. Casserley points out that "from this new point of view it will appear that the doctrine of creation is logically more fundamental than the doctrine of redemption, and that the problem of the Incarnation . . . must be answered in terms of [both doctrines]. . . . The Christ reveals to us not only the fact of human redemption but the purpose of the creation. . . . Incarnational [creationist] theology . . . has been the peculiar . . . characteristic, . . . distinguishing Anglican theology. . . . Duns Scotus . . . held that the purpose of God in creating the world and mankind was one which from the beginning envisaged the incarnation . . . [and] the fulfilment . . . not . . . in the world and in the drama of human existence as we know it, but rather in the Kingdom of God which will issue out of it."[6]

The advantages of this type of theology are that it is closer to the cosmological and eschatological emphases of the New Testament and also that it is not incompatible with the concept of evolution. Speaking to the compatibility of creationist theology and evolution, Casserley notes that "in a very real sense the creation of the world is not yet finished; the process of creation is still going on."[7] He concludes his argument: "It will easily be seen that Christ is interpreted as much more than a Saviour of sinners. He is indeed [that] . . . but He is also the clue to the meaning and purpose of the whole universe." For incarnationalist theology, the scope of theology, its proper sphere of interest, comprehends the entire creation. It is "a catholic theology, . . . a theological account . . . of everything that is or will be."[8]

But the word "redemptive" has another use in much Christian education literature. In this use a semblance of description is alluded to by the user, but in fact the use is highly prescriptive and normative with an unstated premise of appraisal and the purpose of recommending. Crawford illustrates the switch in usage: "The One Unchanging Purpose . . . of the Church always has been, and there is every reason to assume that it always will be, Redemption. The problem is to know just exactly what that means, both in terms of the life of the individual person and the group life increasingly spoken of as the Redemptive Fellowship. . . . Is there danger [these words] may become another cliché? . . . or [is it a meaningful claim?] . . . The stately phrases that the group uses to describe its own life will have meaning only to the degree that they tally with the experience gained in the group relationships. . . . The group life must be such as will give evidence of a purpose to redeem."[9]

Notice the move from the word "redemption," for which some relevant theological data and a reasonable definition can be assembled, to the use of "redemptive" as an adjective in an appraising and recommending way. Further, in answer to his own request for criteria, he offers only an ambiguous notion of "experience gained in group relationships" with "evidence of a purpose to redeem." It is obvious that his hope to avoid a cliché will not be realized. Another might well object, "That is not a redemptive fellowship. The group relationships lack X, or the evidence is not satisfactory to me." To answer, "Oh, but the lack of X or the less than satisfactory evidence does not count against its being a redemptive fellowship, would reveal the judgmental nature of the adjectival use of the word as a slogan to gain approval and to commend a program based upon the implicit value judgment.

Examples of the use of "redemptive" as an adjective in an evaluative or recommending way are easily procured from Christian education foundations sources, and are listed in the alphabetical order of the noun:

1. "redemptive activity"—The church, which is the context for Christian nurture, is the bearer of a redemptive activity which the members have experienced within it. (Cully)[10]
2. "redeeming answers"—The ultimate task of . . . Christian education . . . is to mediate through the church and its ministry God's redeeming answers to man's deepest needs. (Ernsberger)[11]
3. "redeeming Community"—"You are the church, the redeeming community," . . . a divine fellowship, a . . . koinōnia, through which God works in Christ and the Holy Spirit to achieve his purpose of reconcilation. (Zeigler)[12]
4. "redemptive community"—The Christian family has the additional quality of being a redemptive community in which each member brings the forgiving love of God to other saint-sinner members. (Functional Objectives)[13]
5. "redemptive encounter"—Too much emphasis was placed on the transmission of the subject matter of the faith and not enough on redemptive encounter between people and teachers. (Howe)[14]
6. "redemptive experience"—The kērygma yields teaching for the fellowship. . . . It interprets the redemptive experience which it mediates. . . . [Its] nature . . . requires that it be shared. (Cully)[15]
7. "redemptive fellowship"—No single concept is more fundamental . . . in describing the nature of the Church . . . than that of . . . the redemptive fellowship. . . . Unless it is truly a redemptive fellowship in its relationships . . . its voice of redemption will not be heard. (Grimes)[16]
8. "redemptive ministry"—The Christian community as a whole is meant to be the scene of a redemptive ministry to the human self as a whole. (Sherrill)[17]
9. "redemptive mission"—To be a Christian was therefore to

participate in the redemptive mission of Jesus Christ. (Smart)[18]

10. "redemptive needs"—The Word of God is meant to speak through the Church to meet the redemptive needs of people wherever they are regardless of age or circumstance. (Hunter)[19]

11. "redemptive organism"—The church . . . is a redemptive organism. . . . If a particular church does not redeem as well as mediate redemption, it is losing its claim to be the church. (Boehlke)[20]

12. "redemptive power"—It is in the life and work of the lay membership that the Church must manifest in the world its regenerative and redemptive power. (Grimes)[21]

13. "redemptive purpose"—The thing that gives human life its distinction and beauty is the possibility of becoming under God a participant in this redemptive purpose. (Kennedy)[22]

14. "redemptive relationships"—Parents achieve the power to maintain the redemptive and sustaining relationships which are the Gospel in action. . . . The Church's life, when it is truly redemptive, provides a foretaste of the eternal relationship. (Miller)[23]

15. "redemptive witness"—We are seeking to educate for creative and responsible participation in . . . a redemptive witness in the world. (Design)[24]

The above uses of the adjectives "redemptive" and "redeeming" are illustrative of the general tendency in Christian education usage. In the main, the prescriptive-recommending use includes: a designation of the characteristics the redeeming church should possess; normative and homiletical notes in general; slogan-type statements (e.g., "meet the redemptive needs of people"); catchwords for teaching recommendations; arousal and performatory statements; and all seem to suggest that the author has a program, no matter what noun is used, to prescribe under the guise of the "language of redemption."

Of course, there is abundant opinion and some literature to support the notion of the redemptive quality of groups. It ranges from the idea of the acceptance of a person by a group regardless of credentials, called the "gift of life" by Theodore O. Wedel in his article "Group Dynamics and the Church,"[25] to the idea of renewal or the transformation of a person through his participation in small groups, developed by James B. Ashbrook in his article "Theological Dimensions of Renewal Through Small Groups."[26]

That group experiences do inspire many moving and renewing reactions often close to the theological dimension is reported by Wedel from his involvement in the group development laboratory at Bethel, Maine. He noted his chagrin and humiliation on hearing repeatedly in a church-neutral environment, "This is the greatest religious experience of my life."[27]

Ashbrook, in his discussion of the theological implications of small groups, indicates that "the structure of any group is sacred [as opposed to secular] when it is characterized by personal, responsible love."[28] In such a group, encounter and participation are encouraged; and reconciliation, reunion, and renewal are made possible through God's redeeming activity. He also points out that nonchurch groups could qualify as renewal (redemptive) agents.

Ashbrook describes the experience of a disillusioned churchman with a group practicing *koinōnia,* best translated as "community-fellowship-participation." The man had "just about given up any hope of finding anything meaningful in religion."[29] However, Ashbrook reports a vital change in all areas of the man's life as early as two weeks after his coming into the group. Other literature stressing the redemptive nature of groups supports the contentions of both Wedel and Ashbrook.[30]

Nelson's review of the Episcopal Seabury Series mentioned earlier raises a question on the commitment of the series to redemptivism which is relevant here: "Is the church primarily a redemptive fellowship?"[31] The question is seen on closer scrutiny to be a pseudo question. Those who offer and/or accept a prescriptive-normative usage of redemptive will answer the question: "Yes, the church is primarily a redemptive fellowship and the criteria that we have identified will establish the *true* (real, original, etc.) redemptive fellowship." Those who do not accept a normative-prescriptive usage of redemptive will probably say, "No, the church is not primarily a redemptive fellowship. It has a cluster of characterizations, designations, and goals, one of which is redemption."

John E. Skinner asks a similar question in the title of an article that he contributed to *The Living Church:* "How Redemptive Is the Redemptive Fellowship?" Skinner deals not only with the use of the word "redemptive" but also with the commitment under the general area of the "language of redemption" to group process, often called group dynamics. Such a commitment is the concern of this critique, not because churches choose to use certain techniques, but because the justification offered is said to be the fulfillment of redemptive fellowship. Commitment to group process seems hardly ever to be simply a technical or practical issue, as some theorists indicate. The philosophically laden implication is much more complex. Certainly the proper use of group dynamics is a technical and practical issue for the churches to decide in answer to the question, Which methodology seems best? What concerns a philosophical critique the most is the implicit use of the language of redemption to justify the practical issue.

Support for group process as the way to redemptive fellowship is widespread. H. S. Smith prepared the way with his prediction of "a new dynamic in the Church which makes it socially effective and world-redemptive."[32] And the International Council of Religious Education *Guide* commented, "The life of the group is an important part of fruitful Christian education."[33] However, the more extravagant statements are yet to come. S. Little calls the group "a channel for God's work of redemption," and "genuine fellowship where something real happens."[34] G. J. Jud adds that the small group "often becomes in the most real sense the redemptive fellowship of the church."[35]

C. D. Kean quotes Tillich, who "observed that a person is only truly an individual in deciding with which group to identify himself," and goes on to state, "Living the Christian life in these [group] terms is a process of identifying oneself with that fellowship of living men and women in which the Cross of Christ is the dynamic symbol of the members' relationship to God and to each other."[36] And Miller adds that the major goal in the church "is to *become a group*, . . . a community in which each member has a concern for . . . all the others."[37] Grimes offers the opinion that "most Christian nurture does take place within smaller groups," because in them the individual "has been spoken to redemptively, [and he] must then respond in terms of commitment and faith."[38]

Both Sherrill and Hunter offer a justification for the decision to use group process. Sherrill writes: "Methods are indicated which encourage interaction between persons in small groups. The small group in interaction has always played a great part in the life of the church. . . . Small groups intensively interacting commonly appear whenever there is a renaissance of Christian education."[39] And Hunter remarks that "the Church has particular reason to be concerned about truth that pertains to groups. . . . It promised to give us new awareness of the real situation in our group life in the Church. . . . The Parish Life Conference . . . [is a] training operation [in which] the leader asks certain basic questions . . . and supplies very few, if any, answers. . . . But faced with being forced to stay with these questions beyond the usual platitudinous [and inadequate] answers [and use certain group process techniques—role-play, shared leadership, etc.] . . . the conference members are finally driven to a frustration and despair . . . to the point of literally throwing themselves on the mercy of God for understanding and light . . . about the redemptive activity of God in the Church."[40]

It seems hardly necessary to comment on all the above attempts to justify group process as the guarantee of redemptive fellowship; however, Kean's move to unite relationship theology and group process points up a paradox that thwarts analysis and causes much practical confusion. Indeed, as Chaplin observed: "The Church is not redemptive because of its group behavior; God redeems through His worshiping community because it is the Body of Christ."[41] Miller and Grimes both reveal an enthusiasm that is infectious, but on closer examination is seen to be based on only verbal fervor. Sherrill may or may not be historically and methodologically accurate in his attempt at justification, and Hunter can be said to be more homiletically persuasive than theoretically helpful. Thus in the end "redemption" is seen to be a special and stipulative word, as Fry points out, "in the small group mystique . . . to describe alternately the goal and the reality of the small group. . . . God needs small groups in order to do his work. And yet, small groups *must* be redemptive fellowships which only God can create."[42]

Of course, this critique intends no prejudice concerning the use of group dynamics as a practical recourse in any educational situation. Some discrimination, however, must be made between the three definitions of group dynamics offered by Cartwright and Zander in their definitive textbook. First, it is "a sort of . . . ideology concerning the ways in which groups should be organized and managed," with emphasis on democratic leadership, participation, and cooperation, often called "togetherness."

Second, it is "a set of techniques . . . to improve skills in human relations and in the management of groups [role-playing, buzz sessions, observation and feedback of group process, etc.]." This definition is identified most closely with the National Training Laboratory at Bethel, Maine.

Third, it is "a field of inquiry dedicated to achieving knowledge about the nature of groups, the laws of their development and their interrelations with individuals, other groups, and . . . institutions." In this sense it is "a branch of knowledge or an intellectual specialization . . . within the social sciences, [with emphasis on] empirical research for obtaining data on the dynamics of group life."[43]

A study of the literature on the use of group dynamics in Christian education seems to show that most theorists, following the lead of the National Training Laboratory, have adopted the second definition emphasizing the techniques of group process. However, on closer examination, this commitment is seen to be superficial, and a shift to the first definition is revealed. Actually, the theorists are prescribing an ideology not with the political connotation Cartwright and Zander describe but with religious connotations anchored in a metaphysical ontology of being.

It is hardly surprising to note that Cartwright and Zander prefer the third definition. They remark, "Thus conceived, group dynamics need not be associated with any particular ideology concerning the way groups should be organized and managed nor with the use of any particular techniques of group management."[44] The inference they draw is that group dynamics is a tool to be used to gain knowledge about groups and not just a fad to accomplish the ends of "togetherness" or any other ideological notion.

Hardly anyone would deny that group process as a practical, mechanical aid to understanding group behavior has made its place in many and varied fields, and has a role to play in education and religion as a method of describing interpersonal insights and achieving knowledge about groups. But to tag the method with the label of "redemptive fellowship" is moving from the description of group dynamics to an evaluative and prescriptive category laden with philosophical overtones.

The main interest of this chapter has centered about the use of the term "redemptive" as a recommending adjective by Christian education theorists. Of course, there is a common but limited use of "redeem" in the neutral sense of "buying back"; for instance, the redemption of trading stamps. The most common use is the theological sense of "to save [as a redeemer], ransom from sin, or atone for," a usage that most theorists do correctly employ.

The most frequent use of the term "redemptive" in the philosophical foundations of Christian education, however, is as an adjective prescribing the type of group that a group ought to be. Reference to the quality of group process as redeeming (renewing) does not change the use from adjectival/prescriptive, for the author usually designates the characteristics the group should possess; for instance, "personal, responsible love"—and the educational program that will bring it about. Thus the theorists are not seen as describing group process as it is, but prescribing what groups should be like.

Two other philosophical flaws have been revealed by this critique. First, most Christian educators avoid the academically "preferred" definition of group dynamics and effect a combination of the popular definitions—the use of certain techniques to further an ideology concerning ways in which groups should be organized.

Second, most theorists make no effort to resolve the perplexing philosophical paradox of the dualism of existentialist individualism and group life dynamics. The author cited earlier of the Episcopal *Church School Teacher's Workshop* provides a wry concluding comment: "It's this becoming a fuller self . . . somehow in community that intrigues me."[45]

PART THREE

Methodological Decisions

On Teaching

IN THE educative process the primary factors are teaching, learning, (specifically the teacher and the pupil who are teaching and learning), the curriculum (what is being taught), and methodology (how it is being taught). The remaining pages of this work will deal with these educational factors in the order just given. In the overall educative process, teaching and learning are reciprocal activities with reciprocal task descriptions. The task of the teacher is to stimulate learning and the task of the learner is to react to the stimulation provided by the teacher. Such reciprocality enables us to acknowledge two basic educational assumptions: (1) a student will learn from the efforts and art of the teacher—indeed, learning is the goal of teaching; and (2) in teaching and learning an interchange of ideas between teacher and pupil takes place. Of course, we will want to note that the patent duplication by the pupil of the ideas originally enunciated by the teacher and responded to by rote is teaching and learning at its lowest level.

Any consideration of teaching in Christian education must begin with a consideration of the ancient concept of "God as the Teacher." The source of the concept of a divine "Teacher" is the Holy Bible, and especially a passage of Matthew's Gospel, where the author quotes Jesus as exhorting his hearers: "But you must not be called 'rabbi'; for you have one Rabbi [teacher, RSV], and you are all brothers. Do not call any man on earth 'father'; for you have one Father, and he is in heaven. Nor must you be called 'teacher'; you have one Teacher, the Messiah [the Christ, RSV]." (Matt. 23:8–11, NEB.) John also quotes Nicodemus, a Pharisee and member of the Jewish Council as saying: "Rabbi, we know that you are a teacher sent by God" (John 3:2, NEB). Such a reference simply affirms the fact that Jesus as the Son of God and the Second Person of the Trinity participates in the authority and prerogatives of divine teaching. Luke quotes Jesus as he adds the Holy Spirit to the participants in divine instruction, "For when the time comes the Holy Spirit will instruct you" (Luke 12:12, NEB). In fact, John quotes Jesus as promising that the Holy Spirit "will guide you into all the truth" (John 16:13, NEB).

Commentary on the selections from the Bible can be obtained very readily, and it will be discovered that the translation of the key word "rabbi" as "teacher" is accurate. T. W. Manson supports the designation of Jesus as a teacher, noting that it is one of "the two most certain facts in the Gospel tradition."[1] Now, of course, it cannot be known whether Jesus literally intended that no teaching was possible except that supplied by divine intervention, or whether he intended simply to underline the uniqueness of God (the only one true God and Father) and his own uniqueness as a "spiritual leader," which is what many contemporary rabbis are called.

It is obvious that Paul, the first great Christian theologian and bishop, believed that he and other first-century leaders "taught" in the ordinary sense of the word, i.e., performed acts with the intention of instructing. He tells the Corinthians he would shun speaking in an unknown tongue "that by my voice [intelligible speaking] I might teach [instruct, RSV] others" (I Cor. 14:19, KJV). Indeed, Paul ranks teachers third in the work of the church, following behind apostles and prophets, and lists as a criterion for a bishop that he be a good, or as the RSV puts it, an apt, teacher (I Cor. 12:28; I Tim. 3:2, NEB). John and Luke seem to be saying that Christ was an unusually effective and compelling teacher in the material sense, and that the Holy Spirit in some new and unique spiritual sense would also instruct the faithful.

The great churchman-philosopher Augustine asks the question, "Is there one who can be called a teacher?" and answers it with the above quotation from Matthew. He then proceeds to show that the verbal method of a human teacher can never teach the truth, for words or signs do not remind the soul of the truth within, only the "true" (or divine) Teacher can "teach within the pupil" rather than merely "prompting" him externally. Obviously, the "true" teacher is Christ or God.[2] Thomas Aquinas also held that a divine Teacher is necessary to achieve certainty of knowledge available only in the certainty of principles which must come from God. While Aquinas taught that man's highest gift is the light of natural reason, which is in him the likeness and image of God, nevertheless, it is not possible for man to realize his potential for knowing with certainty, even with the help of a human teacher. Thus, to reach the truth, a divine Teacher must be provided. This God has done for us in Jesus Christ.[3] The educational doctrines of Augustine and Aquinas will be considered somewhat more fully in the next chapter, on learning. It will suffice for this chapter to note that if man, even exerting his best, can neither know the truth nor use words or symbols to teach it to others, how can teaching be said to be going on? Or what sort of teaching is being described? Human teaching, therefore, is either impossible or reduced to a mechanical aid (catalytic at best) to turn the pupil to the "real" Teacher—God!

S. F. Bayne, in a paper presented at the Kent School Seminar on the Christian idea of education which he entitled simply "God Is the Teacher," asserted: "The fundamental thought underlying nearly everything that we would want to say about the Christian idea of education is that God is the teacher. It is He who establishes all truth; it is He who wills that men should know the truth; He gives us curious and reflective minds to seek that truth and grasp it and use it; He even gives us the supreme privilege of helping Him in partnership to teach and to learn. But the initiative is His, just as the truth is His; and all teachers . . . do what they do because God, first of all, does what He does." Later he described truth as a thing in itself, speaking for itself: it "takes over; . . . seizes and holds the mind; . . . possesses us, accuses us sometimes, directs us, precisely as if a person were hiding in the truth (as indeed He is)."[4]

Bayne made a point of insisting there is no special "Christian truth" and yet he talked about "Christian teaching" and emphasized a rather special set of tests of "true teaching" "because . . . all teaching must reflect the character of God . . . [and] therefore the Christian teacher [tries] to follow humbly and sincerely in the steps of the great Teacher."[5] Surely Bayne would admit to the contradiction we have pointed out between denying a special Christian category of truth and yet holding to a special Christian category of teaching. Indeed, it would seem that there could be offered substantial support for the rather ordinary language use of "Christian truth" to refer to a body of statements accepted as true by Christianity. Not to be taken seriously philosophically is the personification of truth which Bayne dramatically and homiletically offers in descriptive language using action verbs usually reserved for existent subjects. Of course, auditors familiar with pews "understand" what he is saying, but it will remain happily unknown what the philosophers thought who were present at the Kent School Seminar. Bayne's argument is not as strong as that of either Augustine or Aquinas, because he leaves so much unsupported, e.g.: Is God Truth or does he establish truth? How does he "will" our knowing the truth? Does he literally control the mind's grasping and use of truth, and if so, how? And just how does he work out the teaching partnership? Answers to these questions, and others, of course, must be given before Bayne's notion of "God as teacher" can be given serious consideration as a foundation for an educational program.

Many Christian educators, however, advocate the concept of "God as teacher." Stinnette writes, "In Christian education God is the ultimate teacher."[6] And Wyckoff not only holds that "the real teacher and guide in Christian education is God" but also adds that "the methods of education are those . . . he chooses."[7] Grimes asserts that "God is the real teacher. . . . The [human] teacher must be an agent through whom the pupil is confronted by the living God."[8] *Foundations of Christian Teaching in Methodist Churches* explains that "God is the initiator, the guide, and the sustainer of the process. . . . In the analogy of the dialogue God both initiates the conversation and brings it to fruition."[9] *Basic Principles* summarizes: "There can be no right understanding of Christian teaching, however, without the recognition that it is God who teaches, guides, enlightens. . . . Therefore, we must teach always with a consciousness of limitation. . . . We can at most be instruments."[10] And Ferré concludes, God "teaches by incarnation."[11]

Analysis of the basic concept is restricted if the theorist would have us accept his phrase "God as teacher" purely in ceremonial terms. However, since no restriction is obvious, we justly conclude that the theorists use the concept of a divine source (or person) of teaching as a wedge to introduce and promote certain singular theological and pedagogical doctrines. Of those who propose that the human teacher is agent or instrument, we might well ask, But is he a teacher? Wyckoff's observation about God's choosing the method of education, and Ferré's assignment of "incarnation" as the way God teaches are at the best homiletical enthusiasm and philosophical nonsense.

Other theorists propose the other persons of the Trinity as teacher. Indeed, Cully supports both Christ and the Holy Spirit. In one place she writes that "the gifts of the Spirit . . . shown in teachers, lead children to Christ, the Teacher";[12] and in another place, "The Holy Spirit is the teacher."[13] Karl Barth wrote, "The Holy Spirit . . . is the true and proper *doctor ecclesiae* creating faith as well as giving information and therefore establishing real knowledge."[14] And Ferré adds that the Holy Spirit as Tutor "is finally the teacher of genuine Christian education."[15] *The Functional Objectives for Christian Education* explains that "the learning-teaching act in Christian education is [not] merely a human endeavor. Indeed, what makes the act effective is the way God may use it as a channel for his purposes. . . . The Holy Spirit . . . nurtures Christian persons."[16] And Boehlke concludes, "In this special community, the Holy Spirit acts to motivate people to want to learn the concerns of the Spirit and to accept him as teacher."[17]

Certainly Cully is to be forgiven her contradiction in view

of the general doctrinal confusion attending the Trinity. However, the problem noted earlier remains unsolved: if another person of the Trinity "teaches," how is this effected and what really is the role of the human teacher? Obviously, to be a "channel" is a ceremonial metaphor not meant to apply to actual human activities. Boehlke moves in a circle as he wants the Holy Spirit to prompt persons to want to learn from the Holy Spirit and thus accept him as teacher. And Barth seems to present an impossible dual responsibility to the Holy Spirit who must create faith which will accept information given by the Holy Spirit as "real knowledge."

Some theorists have even named the church as teacher. Wyckoff writes, "The church, the fellowship of Christ's ministry, is also the teacher."[18] Ernsberger notes that "the primary function of the church is to be a teacher."[19] Indeed, Smart argues that "the Church must teach . . . or it will not be the Church. . . . Teaching belongs to the essence of the Church and a church that neglects this function . . . has lost something that is indispensable to its nature."[20] Cully holds that since "the church today is the bearer of a teaching experience, . . . it has itself been taught . . . [and must] teach." The church teaches through worship, the church year, relationships, the church school, and participation in the total life of the Christian community. The church "is sent and therefore teaches."[21] And Ward advised, "Specifically, it is the parish that teaches. . . . Religion is being taught . . . all the time."[22] Naming the church (or parish) as teacher is patently absurd. An institution does hold "teachings," a body of truth which is taught, but to name any institution as "teacher" just cannot be made linguistically sensible, except again in a ceremonial sense, or in the vacuous sense that "everything teaches."

A novel notion of teaching was proposed by Howe, who, moved by an existentialist world view, secured a wide commitment by other theorists to an extremely nonverbal concept of teaching which he called "teaching through the 'language of relationship' as compared to the 'language of words.'" He argues that "meaning is not just behind the word but also in the understanding of the person using the word. . . . People bring meaning out of their experiences in relationship." He uses the words "trust," which "can only be *awakened* in a person," and "love," a "word which looks to personal experiences in relationship to give it meaning." Howe argues that the "language of words" is inadequate for such words, although he admits that "the assumption that teaching is done primarily through verbal communication is still fairly common."[23]

Howe draws on Buber and uses extensively Buber's concept of the I-Thou in his development of a teacher-pupil relationship in Christian education (see Ch. VII). He summarizes his position: "The conception of Christian education that grows out of our thought thus far is one which recognizes that out of the experience in relationship the person brings meaning to his use of the two most important words 'I' and 'Thou' that will help him choose to be in relation to God and others in spite of the meanings in him [and in his environment?] that will drive him to choose against man and God. . . . This may give us a clue to what we mean when we promise to teach. . . . Among other things, the Church promises [in the Sacrament of Baptism] to assume responsibility for the contributions of all relationships to the meanings that this child will bring to his use of these two most important words [I and Thou]. In other words, we make a promise to teach through a relationship of acceptance, as well as by words, . . . [which is] a more appropriate responsibility for the Church . . . since it partakes of the very nature of the Church itself."[24]

Many loose notions and unsupported statements stand out in Howe's writing which beg for analysis. For instance, how can one be certain about the meaning of his experiences in relationship, even if one could give meaning to the words "experiences in relationship"? While there is a high-level meaning of the word "experience," implying matter-of-fact knowledge and empirical reality, Howe's use is strictly low level and may be so vague that it is meaningless, until and unless someone by words gives meaning to feelings and psychophysical responses. Howe has not established the certainty of meanings that he *says* can be brought out of experiences which in themselves are less than reliable evidence, as being in any way superior to the "language of words." His term, the "language of relationship," therefore, must be considered a "slogan title" naming a package of slogans and a type of enthusiastic and end-means program for a certain sort of activity within the church. "Trust" and "love," which he claims are good examples of the use of his "meaning method," are chameleon-like words, almost unknowable and undefinable, yet Howe never discriminates on either word. Further, his conception of Christian education as one which will bring *from* relationship meanings *of* relationship to help one choose to be *in* relationship is so trivial in its circularity that any attempt to explicate the notion would fail. Howe's summary is merely a sort of peroration, and his promise to supply a clue as to "what we mean when we promise to teach" brings forth only relationship slogans.

Mary Jane Aschner, in the volume *Language and Concepts in Education,* discusses the question of why a theory of language is important in the analysis of teaching. She points out that "language is both the instrument and the vehicle of teacher-student interaction. . . . Day-to-day activities are sustained almost entirely in talk. . . . Of course, there are occasional periods of [other activities]. . . . But whenever class is 'in session,' . . . their activities are essentially and typically verbal. . . . Observation thus bears out the fact that the conduct of classroom instruction is inescapably involved in the use and interpretation of language—written, printed, and above all, spoken." Aschner presents what she calls "an action concept of language" drawing upon Ludwig Wittgenstein's "language games" in which the pattern or "rules" are maintained in the acts of saying or telling, and in all forms of verbal interaction. Her conclusion is especially practical. She calls attention to the dual use of language by the teacher. "First, he acts with language, using it in the performance of almost all those actions describable as teaching. Secondly, . . . he observes what his pupils say and do under instruction . . . in order . . . to diagnose and adapt his teaching to the pupils' present state of comprehension and progress in learning. . . . Moreover, it is the teacher's task and purpose *not* to condition the responses or the learnings of his pupils, but to develop in them their own capacities to think and act responsibly."[25]

The importance of linguistic expressions in teaching is also underlined by B. O. Smith. The teacher will be able to learn much about his students from their use of language, which, along with certain "natural signs" (posture, tone of voice, and facial expression) can reveal "his emotional state, the grammatical and linguistic [also the logical and factual] errors he makes, whether or not he understands something, the values he holds." Using this information, the teacher can act intelligently. Of course, the teacher also expresses himself to his students through the vehicle of language. In fact, teaching can hardly be said to occur without linguistic activities, as the teacher "makes assignments, gives directions, explains events and statements, interprets words and other expressions, proves propositions, justifies decisions and actions, makes promises, praises and blames students."[26]

Komisar also supports language as the predominant factor in teaching. He concludes, "There is nothing that is teaching but that talking makes it so." Noting that teaching (1) names an occupation or an activity; (2) refers to a general enterprise; (3) characterizes an act, he further categorizes "teaching acts" as (a) "Learning-Donor Acts" (producing learning); (b) "Learning-Enhancing Acts" (maintaining learner's fit state); and (c) "Intellectual Acts," among which he lists explaining, interpreting, justifying, and proving.[27] In another place Komisar argues that "teaching is characterized by the overall rationality it seeks to foster in the student." Its aim is "producing understanding."[28] Scheffler agrees, noting that "in teaching, the teacher is revealing his reasons for the beliefs he wants to transmit and is thus, in effect, submitting his own judgment to the critical scrutiny and evaluation of the student." Teaching, then, is dialogue which he later calls "an initiation into the rational life."[29]

Hunter suggests another unique notion of teaching as he insists that "a case can be made for using *train* rather than *teach*. . . . The basic meaning of *teach* is to impart knowledge or skill, whereas to *train* is to make proficient by instruction and practice. The difference . . . is significant for those who give a central place to engagement. *Training* definitely involves proficiency and practice. *Teaching* . . . is more specifically related to communicating knowledge about something. . . . If we are preparing a person to do something ["confront and react to (God in) the deepest process at work in . . . soul . . . and . . . life"] it is rather appropriate to think in terms of training."[30] In holding this position, Hunter cuts himself off from both existentialist and pedagogical support. Dr. Ralph Harper, for instance, insists that "when one trains another, he evokes innate powers by displaying his own. . . . [It is] a matter of enslavement in humans, whereas it is natural in animals. . . . The human being will . . . want to know . . . a reason for doing it, . . . an explanation."[31]

Examples in other fields can be found to help with "train" and "teach." Mountain climbers who already "know" about mountain climbing assemble to be trained in (to practice) the actual climbing. Men are taught medicine first and then given practice (training) later as interns. Nurses are said to be trained because of the preponderance of practical activity in their program. Indeed, in both medicine and nursing, the cry is for more teaching and, interestingly enough, in the abstract fields of knowledge. What Hunter implies by his choice of "training" is either naïveté, that persons know enough about their religion to justify some type of advanced program; or enthusiasm, that his type of "training" will provide both theory (knowledge) and practice (proficiency).

Smart asks the important question, "What, then, is teaching? Teaching essentially . . . addresses itself to the situation of the man who has repented and turned to God and to the situation of children of believers who through the influence of their parents have in them a measure of faith, even though they have also . . . unbelief. . . . God has established a function of teaching . . . that his work of grace may take place. . . . We teach so that through our teaching God may work in the hearts of those whom we teach. . . . The key . . . is the teacher . . . who showed us the way of faith, and helped us to take our first faltering steps along it."[32] Unfortunately, Smart never does answer his original and provocative question. He speaks of a highly specialized "situation" in a context where his overall slogan of "Teach for Discipleship" will provide both content and method for his design for Christian education. His specialization is seen in another position, "Good teaching has in it the note of the preacher's proclamation . . . and should have the expectation of producing a transformation of life."[33]

Finally, it is thoroughly confusing to confront the many notions of teaching and the identifications of the role of teacher in the writings of the Christian educators. No wonder laymen are critical and apathetic as they seek to understand and appreciate education in the Christian churches. Teaching is called "nurture" and preparation "for personal encounter" by Grimes; "participating in lives" by Ross Snyder; "guiding persons in group process" by *Foundations;* "creating right conditions" in *How to Score in Sunday School Work;* "confrontive leadership" by *Workbook: Developing Your Educational Ministry;* "relationships" by Miller; and "fellowship" by Vieth.[34] A teacher in church education is exhorted to be a "midwife" ("the teacher . . . strives to bring truth to birth in the learner") by Stinnette; a "minister" and a "theologian" by Smart; a "two-way communicator" by Sherrill; an "encourager" by Chaplin; a "surrogate parent" by Yeaxlee; a "sculptor of the spirit" by Kennedy; a "trainer" by Hunter; and an "I" to the pupil's "thou" and a "thou" to the pupil's "I" by Howe.[35]

On analysis, the several notions appearing under the heading of "teaching" in the writings of Christian educators are all seen to be theoretically confusing and empirically impracticable. For instance, in spite of its long history and its estimable list of supporters, the notion of "God as teacher" fails, since in the end human teachers do the teaching and the role of the human teacher must be explicated. Is he a deluded puppet or merely a mechanical intermediary? Furthermore, the concept of divine teaching awaits a prior epistemological decision, How to know? If the answer is only by revelation and the mysterious will and activity of God, then the answer is beyond the canon available to all rational men. Of course, such a dilemma points to the prescriptive nature of the notion; divine teaching is based on a theological commitment and leads to many strange concepts, e.g., the church as teacher.

The other unique notions also fall short of the performatory and intentional sense of teaching. The notion of "teaching through the language of relationship" (nonverbal experiences in relationship) as compared to the language of words is at best an uncritical enthusiasm of an existentialist theological commitment. But words are necessary to discuss meaning, even the meaning of experience. Indeed, since words are both its instrument and vehicle, teaching can hardly occur without them. All attempts to identify teaching in terms of learning and the experience to be imparted, (the experiential notion, sometimes discussed as "faith encountered" or "dealing with religious issues") fail because they are prescriptive and not descriptive as they are advertised. The substitution of "training" for "teaching" adds nothing to a serious consideration of teaching. As a matter of fact, training is often mentioned as the lowest usage of teaching, e.g., "animals are trained." At best, training refers to a preponderance of practical activity, e.g., a trained nurse.

Finally, Christian education theorists err mainly because they fail fully to take into account a serious consideration of the art of teaching—what is actually done when one teaches. As B. O. Smith points out, "He who would improve an art must first understand it . . . not with loose abstractions, but with systematic and painstaking analysis of that art . . . [of] the facts of teaching—of what it is that we actually do when we teach . . . the linguistic and symbolic nature of the teaching process, and the fundamental role of logical operations in teaching."[36] It is all too easy to forget to include the main reason for arranging an educational program, that most essential element, teaching—the education of another person or persons. The teacher either teaches (performs certain acts in the practical, skillful manner of an artisan) with the intention of producing not scale models or imitators, but persons who, by and because of their education, have a wider knowledge, broader appreciations, and increasing experience in making value decisions, or he is not teaching at all.

CHAPTER X

On Learning

IN THE last chapter we identified teaching and learning as reciprocal activities with reciprocal task descriptions. Now we must make a further effort to distinguish between these two concepts often described as having an assimilative relationship. While it is perfectly true that teaching involves some effort to accomplish learning, the converse is not necessarily true. Indeed, the ancient slogan "There can be no teaching without learning" has been unmasked by analytic philosophy as an attractive attention getter to specify the child as the center of the teacher's interest and concern. Furthermore, the usual analogy of teacher-learner, seller-buyer entailment of "results" has also been shown to be limited and trivial.[1] Another difference between teaching and learning is suggested in the distinction often made between "task" words (to express activities) and "achievement" (or success) words (to express accomplishment). Thus "teaching" is a task word and "learning" is a success word.

B. O. Smith is quite severe in his separation of learning from teaching. "We do not even use the hyphenated expression teaching-learning . . . to signify . . . result[s]. . . . It is superfluous; . . . [or] . . . to indicate . . . where there is learning, there is teaching; . . . [or] to mean that teaching always results in intended learning. . . . Such is not the case. . . . The word 'teaching' . . . is used to refer to what the teacher does rather than to the behavior of the student or to what happens to him as a result of instruction."[2] Obviously, one sense of learning is provided by the performance of the learner.

Two questions dominate discussions on the concept of learning: What do we mean by learning? and How do people learn? The first question requires an analysis of the concept of learning as it appears in ordinary educational talk, while the second question suggests an appeal to science, or at least to psychology, for a mechanical process in which that phenomenon happens which is usually described as learning. Unfortunately, far too many uncritical educators follow the psychologist and make educational decisions based on his findings. The unfortunate part of this blind discipleship of psychology on the part of educators is that while psychologists are interested in learning, their interest is centered in mechanical or extratheoretical variables in a process. Komisar has identified two "referring" uses of learning, "as the *process* of regularizing a response and as the *product* of the response so regularized." Learning as process/product is offered as a technical explanation of how people learn, but it is just not enough to cover the entire concept of learning. According to Komisar: "In the assertion 'He [a person has now] learned,' we are neither referring to a process nor a product. . . . [It is] a performative utterance . . . to announce success."[3]

Noting the apparent "tyranny of [educational] fashion by psychology," Peters charges that "the fact is very little of learning theory [supplied by psychology] is of much interest or relevance to the educator . . . [and] there is little in psychology that good teachers do not know already."[4] As a matter of fact, Peters claims that "learning theory [psychology] has a great deal to learn from the study of the practice of education. . . . The careful experimental study of situations under which human beings learn all sorts of things rather than by a concentration on highly artificial situations where rats and dogs [and pigeons] learn very limited things."[5] Best also cautions against another naïve habit of educators who accept the prescriptions of psychologists based on the descriptions of their "experiments" in spite of the lack of a "valid 'line of reasoning' from . . . descriptive statements . . . to [the] prescriptive utterance, 'children should be taught.' "[6]

In the general field of Christian education, a review of the classical literature on the concept of learning seems to be a prerequisite to the consideration of the modern theories. Perhaps the first full-blown classical concept of learning offered by a Christian was that of Augustine of Hippo (354–430). Augustine was a Platonist and developed his most important educational doctrines under the influence of Plato, i.e., the doctrine of divine illumination, which posits that truth is latent in the inner man, the rational soul, and Christian education merely reminds the soul of the truth already there. He challenged the traditional "transmission" theory, insisting that no one is stupid enough to expect his son to learn only what the teacher thinks. In other words, learning is something more than the reception and cognition of words or signs, but for Augustine that something more in learning is supplied only by God who provides the light in which truth can be known.[7]

Thomas Aquinas, although obviously familiar with and respectful of the views and the writings of Augustine, had nevertheless rejected Platonism in favor of Aristotelianism. Aquinas talked of learning as an actualization of the potentiality inherent in every individual. His learning theory is based on the Aristotelian doctrine of act and potential and cause, to which he added his own theological development of Aristotle's thought. Because man is always a potential knower he needs only the act of teaching to serve as a catalyst to activate the learning phenomenon of actualization within.[8]

Since both Augustine and Aquinas have greatly influenced Christian education in Roman Catholic and Protestant churches, some critique of their learning theories must be offered. Both churchmen are agreed that the pupil must learn more than the conclusions imparted to him by his teacher by way of language. Indeed, in both Augustine and Aquinas, learning is toward an absolute truth or certainty which is God, and without God's direct intervention the activity called learning will stop short of either truth or certainty. Of course, the question here is, What sort of learning is this, which Augustine and Aquinas are describing? Indeed, if, as both churchmen agree, truth and certainty come only from God, yet are also the goal of learning, which is a process supplied by God, how can man be said to learn in any sense that is human and verifiable? In the pedagogical and everyday use of the word, Augustinian and Thomistic learning is not possible.

In modern Christian education literature, abundant consideration of the concept of learning is obvious, but equally obvious is the confusion both of definition and use. In answer to the question What do we mean by learning? the following definitions were proposed. Learning is:

"entering upon a personal relationship with Jesus Christ" (Smart)

"Christ-like responses to actual situations" (ICRE)

"participation in God" (Ferré)

"a radical transformation of the self" (Boehlke)

"mastering developmental tasks" (R. J. Havighurst)

"participative knowledge and insight" (Stinnette)

"change" (*Age Group Objectives*)

"the process of life changing [and] of human becoming" (*Design*)

having " 'learned' what they have become" (Sherrill)

being "caught up in the dynamic currents of group thinking" (S. Little)[9]

And the answers to the question How do we learn? has elicited the following comments. We learn:

"through life" (G. E. Koehler)

"in every activity" (ICRE)

"through participation" (Zeigler)

"through involvement" (Wyckoff)

as we "experience what is being taught" (P. B. Maves)

"by the way we are treated" (Miller)

"in relationship [a relational experience]" (Boehlke)

"where we love [to learn we must love]" (Stinnette)

"psychologically [not logically]" (*Functional Objectives*)

"through personal and creative encounter" (Grimes)

as we "begin with needs that the learners *recognize* as needs" (Ernsberger)

through a "group-centered experience" (Cully)[10]

The condition represented by these selected definitions and explanations is universal. More than one hundred books and articles were consulted to establish the chaotic nature of the discussion of learning in Christian education noted above.

The *International Journal of Religious Education* (author unknown), in an essay "How Do We Learn?" calls the key question not "What shall we teach?" nor "What shall we learn?" but, "What, by God's grace, shall we become together?" A description of learning is offered: "[It] involves change and change can take place when a group or individual is faced with an interest, a need, a problem, a tension, or a question . . . [and] a learning activity can be selected and undertaken." The article says that five learning actions or steps are identifiable. The first is "listening to the gospel and responding to it in faith and love." Unfortunately, the remaining steps are not clearly "identifiable," but have to do with a practical application to life of the "gospel light," which it is claimed will widen interests, meanings, values, and responsibilities, and somehow is part of a "program for persons to live with and through these dynamically related experiences."[11]

The bulk of the content of this article is educational nonsense! The question "What, by God's grace, shall we become together?" may be an important question to one committed to a theological position, but it is not a substitute for an inquiry into the concept of learning. The attempt to make learning meaningful never quite comes off. The kind of change prescribed is not made clear and the relaxed recommendation to select and undertake a "learning activity" to meet the interests, needs, etc., would create sheer chaos in any educational situation. The promised identification of "learning steps" never becomes that, but degenerates into homiletical clichés, e.g., "responding . . . in faith and love," and a " 'program' for persons to live with."

Sherrill, defining learning as "changes in persons which take place . . . within the encounter" seems to include even physiological changes as well as "the deeper changes" in the self noted by psychology "when persons interact in true two-way communication." He concludes: "These changes *are* the content of the learning. . . . The motifs of the selves [the typical response of self to others], . . . their ability to perceive meaning, the spiritual or demonic nature of the interaction, and the nature of the symbols with which they communicate with one another—all these are relevant to the question of the responses . . . and the changes in selves which will take place."[12] Obviously, Sherrill has chosen to place his consideration of "learning" firmly in the camp of psychology, but his move into depth psychology and relationship theology removes his explanation from philosophical consideration. Two major obstacles are his definition of "change" as "redemption" and his reference to the "demonic nature of interaction."

Ferré poses an interesting definition of learning as "a process of free experience within which alone love can become real." He continues: "All life is a school. The whole purpose of creation is learning . . . to complete our own cosmic education. . . . At his mother's breast he [man] learns what God's school is like. The breast represents nature; the mother's face, history. . . . He learns . . . both to become dependent upon nature [on nature's breast] and history [the face of history]."[13] Ferré's definition reveals his metaphysical preoccupation and his theological commitment. However, his elucidation of "God's school" is interesting as a mystical, poetic analogy, but unbelievable as an educational notion, and beyond serious analysis as either fact or concept.

Stinnette also reaches beyond the ordinary context with his comment, "To ask what it means to learn anything is to ask the deeper question, what is the meaning of history?" The difficulty here is simply that the conditional question is not a matter-of-fact decision, but a matter of appraisal and depends in the end on the point of view of the speaker. Therefore, to learn means what Stinnette says it means, i.e., "living into that identity which is already present in the world in Jesus Christ. . . . For the Christian, learning is 'Christomorphic,' . . . transfiguration, . . . man's appropriate response to God's action . . . which engages our hearts as it radically transforms." We learn "through commitment and encounter" where we love. The prescriptive nature of Stinnette's thesis is quite obvious, man "learns" to become "what he already is in the mind of God,"[14] aided by the revealed Christ. This process is what he calls "transfiguration" or "participatory knowledge"—the "incarnational" interpretation of the Bible account in order to participate in the event.

Grimes holds a similar position: "The most significant learning occurs through the experience we may call *personal and creative encounter.* From a Christian point of view, nothing has really been learned until it affects one personally [existentially] in terms of his relationships. . . . [It] involves, at least on its deeper levels, this personal encounter between the learner . . . and the Lord of Life." In another place he writes, "We need to take seriously the small group . . . where the life of Christian dialog [and communion] may occur . . . [and] Christian learning is most likely to occur."[15] Little supports Grimes, noting that "educators believe that real learning occurs when persons are caught up in the dynamic currents of group thinking [study]." Group learning "achieves a permanence it would not otherwise have. [The] new way of life is rooted in a fellowship which upholds that way."[16] Of course, in a trivial sense Grimes is quite right, learning is a personal matter, but Grimes means much more than this. The key words are "existential" and "relationships," which transform the discussion from available categories for analysis to those of theological presupposition. The notion of personal encounter with Jesus Christ is explored elsewhere, but learning theory dependent on primary, face-to-face relations is bound to be imprecise and prescriptive. Both Grimes and Little prescribe group process as the most lively hope for Christian or, to use Little's adjective, "real" learning. But what comes through is scarcely more than their recommendation of a method with little or no evidence for its support.

Boehlke struggles bravely but vainly to achieve his stated aim of a Christian "learning theory." His definitions of learning involve a commitment to relationship theology, and his definition of "theory" as "that attempt to summarize succinctly what has occurred and what ought to occur" is just not enough. A theory in the strong sense of the word is a verified hypothesis or a set of hypotheses that explain or demonstrate their subject matter. (See O'Connor for a full discussion of theories and explanations.)[17] Boehlke rejects "rote memorization" as "not Christian learning because the meanings . . . are always relative to the quality of relationships with persons." He notes, however, that "man as spirit must learn the things of the Spirit through the life of God as Spirit. [The concerns of learning] are learned in the Spirit or they are not learned at all." Boehlke calls his theory of learning "creation-engagement"—"creation" to involve divine participation and "engagement" to signify the "whole person." Actually, "God grasps the learner and gives him the insight to perceive wider implications of the revelation received. . . . Without God's creative work, human learning is never able to go beyond the reaches of man's mind. . . . God reorganizes the learner's perceptual processes."[18]

Boehlke's discussion of learning is cliché-ridden, e.g., "the whole person." He resorts to slogans at will and cites as evidence highly conceptual notions, e.g., God "reorganizing" perceptual processes. His assignment of the accomplishment of Christian nurture to the Holy Spirit is also questionable. In a ceremonial sense it can be said that for the Christian "spiritual matters" are known by "spiritual means." By this is meant some devotional or mystical concepts explained *sui generis*. But Boehlke goes all the way, including knowledge (without restriction), attitudes, skills, etc., in his list of concerns learned only "in the Spirit." Obviously, this latter claim cannot be supported. His own theory fails in the same dimension. He wants to put the person in the learning, but in the end makes God responsible for that learning. It is almost impossible to conceive of human learning which is "able to go beyond the reaches of man's mind." Learning is either human learning with mental and verbal characteristics, or it is not learning in any communicable sense.

Hunter also uses the term "engagement," and notes that the Episcopal Seabury Series had espoused a "new theory of learning" which "emerged as a direct product of the theological assumptions of the program. These assumptions began with the declaration that what is being communicated in Christian education is the gospel, that the communicator is God himself, and that the context of this communication is the covenant community, the Body of Christ.

"There was nothing particularly new in these theological assumptions. The problem was that thus far in Christian education they had not produced a learning theory with indisputable antecedents. . . .

"What did this mean in terms of a theory of learning? For the builders of this particular program it meant that the learning they sought, the apprehension of the gospel, would be most likely to occur through maintaining an adequate balance of past, present, and future. In short, they believed that the gospel is encountered and is most likely to be responded to through a balanced exposure to the meaning of God's historic action and his action now in people's lives, with due consideration to the eschatological nature of God's action in all history. This theory of learning had a powerful and determining effect upon the shape of the program as curriculum builders faced the traditional problems that had to be solved."[19]

Hunter's explication of Seabury "learning" is an illustration of the basic problem in the philosophical and methodological foundations of Christian education. Christian education cannot ignore the "learning theories" of general education save at the cost of the sacrifice of educational research and studies. Unique learning theories are often little more than propagational or dogmatic prescriptions. And, of course, Hunter's theory is not new. Actually, it is a restatement of Biblical-Augustinian-Thomistic theories which hold that God provides the content of all learning, a notion dependent in the end on *sui generis* support.

Further, Hunter is seen to be self-contradictory when he argues that "we do not learn secular truth one way and religious truth another. . . . Both the occurrence of learning and the integration of learning depend upon the eventual coalescence of four elements of experience . . . : 1. Immediate personal encounter; 2. Identification of the encounter; 3. Symbolization of experience; 4. The ordering of experience. . . . These four elements . . . are not . . . peculiar to religious knowledge or Christian education."[20] Hunter's reference to experience as basic to the occurrence of learning should be a warning to recall the trivial and circular meaning of "learning by experience" as either "learn by learning" or "experience by experiencing." Yet Hunter opts for such learning. He calls for instruction not "essentially geared to subject matter, or detached learning," but to "immediate Christian nurture."[21]

Hunter does give some examples of learning under his theory: first, of a child who burns his hand on a hot stove, and second, of a man who must make a moral decision. Obviously, the examples are not at all equal learning situations. The first example was the concern of Plato, Leibniz, and Locke, to name just a few, and still this so-called simple type of learning remains unexplained. The second example is so highly normative that only prescriptive-evaluative statements attach to it— hardly a claim for an "experience" criterion except in the special religious sense which we have examined elsewhere.

Returning to the unique theological presuppositions of his learning theory, Hunter argues that the "fundamental nature of religious learning . . . pertains to God's action. God is the source of this learning, and God is an essential force in the operation." If this is true, then to learn anything one must go to the source, a task in which Augustine's concern for human learning underlines the nonempirical, conceptual nature of the hope for Christian education. Hunter does indicate the metaphysical nature of this hope by suggesting that persons may respond to God's action even though they may not understand. "Where understanding is possible it is a necessary ingredient for Christian learning, but where it is not possible, then other ingredients suffice," e.g., "love."[22] Overlooking the necessity for defining the learning which he calls Christian, Hunter certainly owes his readers a full explanation of the "other ingredients" he says can substitute for understanding in learning. For instance, how can "love" be seriously considered as an

"ingredient" in learning except as a psychological (noncogni-
tive) element in the environment?

Hunter's description of his learning theory as "theologically
rooted" is a clue to its patent indoctrinational rather than its
announced scientific intention. "If we use these four elements
of learning in understanding and categorizing the nature of
man's response to God, it then becomes possible to say that
Christian learning involves an awareness of the action of God
within our lives, a recognition of the religious issues which
are created by God's action and our response, a relating of this
experience and these religious issues to the mighty acts of God
in the past, and, finally, some comprehension of the relationship
which this experience or symbol has to the whole body of
Christian revelation and Christian experience."[23]

Miller supports Hunter in suggesting that when the Bible
is taught theologically, trained teachers who identify themselves with man's sin and judgment and also with the new life
of redemption will "discover how to communicate the saving
truth of God."[24] At no point does Miller explain how man can
"discover" (learn) by himself the theological concepts he is
asked to "communicate" (teach), e.g., "sin and judgment,"
"the new life of redemption." Perhaps such discovery (learning) and communication (teaching) is the message of ecclesiastical authority about these concepts with the necessary
explication and exhortation to pass them on. Without prior
theological commitments, comments on such learning and
teaching are just not meaningful in any public sense.

Several questions have arisen during our critique of the
concept of learning in Christian education. However, on further examination, they narrow down to a single question, Are
the programs for education espoused by the theorists in Christian education theories of learning in any sense at all? Or are
they attempts, albeit in another guise, to indoctrinate a certain
"apprehension of the gospel . . . encountered and responded to
through . . . God's historic action . . . now in people's lives?"[25]
Actually, this special learning is an answer to "learning how"
but in a *sui generis* sense only. A few theorists have restated

Augustinian-Thomistic learning doctrines noting that the goal of learning is truth, which is God, and that it is accomplished by a process of divine "illumination" or "actualization" supplied by God. Thus learning is removed from the consideration of men armed only with human canons and criteria of verification.

Another discomforting note is the rejection of all other learning theories in favor of a unique theory. Since there is no special religious learning, a unique theory in religious education will be highly prescriptive. For instance, "learning how to reach God" sounds like a grand and superior goal for an educative process within the Christian church, until it becomes necessary to translate it into an educational program. To accomplish it would require a teacher who had indeed "reached God," a curriculum methodology structured to match, and research studies to support an independent theory of learning. The fact is that unique religious learning theories are little more than attempted justifications for value and theological judgments made prior to and thus determinative of an announced theory of learning.

Other items of interest in the critique on learning are: (1) the failure of most theorists to discriminate adequately between the concepts of teaching and learning (So often the simple discrimination of teaching as what the teacher does, and learning as the performance of the learner, is obliterated); and (2) the recurring notion of "learning by experience." In general educational literature, it was noted, the notion is both trivial and circular. And any attempt to add to it a special religious sense, e.g., the "discovery" of Biblical truth, or "seeing Jesus as his contemporaries saw him," leads only to prescriptivity based on the theological positions espoused. Indeed, the frank admission of many theorists is that their unique theory of learning is based on prior theological commitments. A special Christian theory of learning is thus concluded to be theoretically unsupportable and impracticable.

CHAPTER XI

On Curricula and Methodology

THE EDUCATIVE process is commonly held to describe the interrelation of three essential elements: the teacher, the pupil, and the curriculum, the presence of which distinguishes formal education from conversation or "just living." Since the preceding chapters have considered the teacher and the pupil (teaching and learning), we turn now to a consideration of curricula, which is a name given to that special process whereby an educational program is organized and presented. P. H. Phenix has pointed out that "a complete description of the curriculum has at least three components: (1) *what* is studied—the 'content' or 'subject matter' of instruction—(2) *how* the study and teaching are done—the 'method' of instruction—and (3) *when* the various subjects are presented—the order of instruction."[1] Historically, of course, the most vital questions have been *what* and *when,* not *how.* Of late, however, there is an increasing interest in how! This chapter will concern itself, first, with a definition of curricula as well as with an analysis of the question What do Christian education theorists mean by curricula?; second, with the question entertained in any consideration of curricula: What methodology should be used? and, more precisely, Is there any unique methodology that can be termed "Christian education methodology"?

Educators have defined "curricula" in a number of different ways, ranging from nebulous "life experiences" to "all the activities presented by the educator and engaged in by the pupil." A thorough analysis of this concept in educational literature would be fruitful! Broudy provides the helpful observation that the "curriculum problem" consists of several distinctions: (1) the difference between the experience provided and the outcome of it; (2) the differences in "intervening processes" internal to a pupil (perceiving, remembering, etc.); (3) the difference in "school outcomes and life outcomes [transfer]." Broudy exposes the theoretical problem of curricula, noting that "controversies over the curriculum are arguments about the *kinds* of experience the pupil shall have in the classroom during his school life."[2] Phenix explains that the curriculum problem is one of economy. He remarks that humans are limited in capacity and there is simply too much to know; therefore, we use a curriculum to economize on potential and make the wisest selection of study content. "Human intelligence is too rare and precious a thing to squander on a haphazard program of instruction."[3]

Turning to the field of Christian education, one may observe that a brief review of the literature reveals several broad definitions of curricula. The broadest definition available is that of J. D. Butler, who gave it in the hope "that this will avoid the implication that all of curriculum is study literature. . . . For education generally, the curriculum is constituted by all of those influences and media of communication by which the less mature are nurtured in the culture of the community of which they are a part." And curricula in Christian education "is also constituted by all of those media of communication and all those influences by which the less mature are nurtured within the Christian community and, it is hoped, brought into effective relation to God and made partakers of the body of Christ." He does admit, however, that "there is a sense in which the Bible, . . . theology, . . . theologizing, . . . [and] those who teach are curriculum." Further, Butler also gives what he calls "a narrow definition" of curricula in Christian education as, "the study materials deliberately designed and prepared as a [the] central agent . . . in the Christian nurture of children, youth and adults, . . . also particular courses or programs of study as well as a study literature."[4]

The *International Journal of Religious Education*, however, underlines the "broader" definition in an article, "Curriculum Is Custom-Made," emphasizing the influence of all the relations and experiences that help persons grow in Christian faith. "The curriculum includes all that the church and family do to confront persons with the message of God in Christ and calls them to their true life in relation with God and their fellows . . . [also] what the Church does to persons in its whole life—in its own building, but also in its families and in the community."[5]

Butler and the *Journal* share the shortcoming of offering more of a preachment than a definition. Butler's "broader" definition is ambiguous as he fails to clarify and analyze "nurture" and "the Christian community" (a synonym for "culture"?), and as he adds the homiletical exhortation of purpose which also fails to define. The *Journal* fails to provide clear and supported justification for "how persons grow in Christian faith" and offers only a little homily for what the author thinks Christian education ought to be doing. Butler's "narrow" definition seems to be closer to the model concept of curriculum in secular education—it has structure, scope, and sequence— even though his goal of nurturing the less mature in the culture of the community needs explication and analysis.

Of course, the literature abounds with definitions of curricula. The following quotations are representative of the theoretical confusion which at times causes the outsider to believe that there are as many educational theories as there are theorists. The curriculum of Christian education is:

1. The experience of the learner under guidance, . . . a series of activities which lead the learner into the enrichment and control of life experience, . . . [and] is as inclusive as life itself. (*Curriculum Guide*)[6]
2. Used as a name for educational program . . . [and] includes all those activities and experiences which are initiated or utilized by the church for the achievement of the aims of Christian education. (Vieth)[7]
3. All those experiences which are a part of Christian growth and change. (Ernsberger)[8]
4. [That which deals] with total experience of the person in the church. (Kennedy)[9]

5. The plan by which the church and home undertake to fulfill their obligations for the task of Christian nurture. (Wyckoff)[10]

6. The total meaning of all that happens: words, relationships, deeds, action, participation. The curriculum is, in the final analysis, what the person takes home with him. (Grimes)[11]

7. The dynamic process in which people discover the values that make their life meaningful. . . . Valid educational resources must grow out of this process. (Braun)[12]

8. Recommendations and "for instances" described in the hope that they will stimulate the planning of ministries uniquely suited to each congregation. (*Workbook*)[13]

9. An overall plan or design for providing particular types of experiences that, it is hoped, will bring the pupil into the presence of God and encourage him to respond to God in faith, love, and understanding. (*Foundations*)[14]

10. [And Dorothy Scott is reported to have said that she saw] curriculum being lived rather than spoken.[15]

A review of these several definitions reveals the general and patent ambiguity. "Experience [life itself]," "activities," "dynamic process," "all that happens," and "for instances," are just not enough to support anything but highly singular and unique curricula. The use of the special terms and aims of Christian education fails to inform the ambiguity, e.g., "Christian growth and change," "Christian nurture," "people discover the values that make their lives meaningful," and "ministries uniquely suited to each congregation." On examination, these are seen to be homiletical and in need of special grounding in a theological context. Miss Scott is simply confused as to what she was in fact observing; as a matter of fact, a curriculum is hardly "lived" or "spoken"; it is both a concept (a theory of what is to be taught) and a program (the materials and sequence of the teaching).

Hunter offers a justification for the Episcopal Seabury Series decisions in curriculum-building, arguing that the problem of Christian education is characterized "by three inescapable choices . . . of emphasis, . . . so decisive as to amount virtually to an either-or choice." He identifies these choices as: (1) "the choice between preparing people for the future *and* ministering to them where they are now"; (2) the choice between "culture transmission" and "culture change," "between making paramount the task of transmitting culture and enabling a child to become a part of the Christian process which changes culture"; (3) the choice between the development of a motivation based on a "man-dependent" and a "grace-dependent" response, "a dependency choice, one which pertains to what we believe to be the source of our ability to do things."[16]

A consideration of Hunter's "problem choices" will be made in reverse order since in that order they represent theological, sociological, and educational decisions. Hunter identifies the third or "man-dependency" choice as the Pelagian heresy. "The idea that man . . . is so filled with latent goodness and strength that he can do all things through himself if only his will and determination are strong enough." Of course, the problem here is not methodological but theological. It is at best a judgment: "I choose to emphasize human will." Hunter's concern for expressions of Pelagianism which produce "results that are more to be feared than acknowledged atheism itself" is overdramatic and factually unsupported.[17] Further, his examples are not at all convincing. Staff authors could have written similar examples with opportunity for rebuttal to explain meanings and contexts.

Hunter himself provides a bit of heterodoxy (in bold contradiction to his stand here) in his later position calling for human interest and findings "dependent not only on revelation but also upon trained observation and interpretation for an understanding of man and his situation."[18] His concern for "Does [Seabury Christian education] . . . center in man or in God?" was answered "man" by many of the early Seabury critics.[19] His other question illustrates the void or the meaninglessness of this criterion for curricula, "Is it chiefly a matter of morals, of doing what we ought to do—or is it a matter of looking to God?" Is this a valid question? What could be expected to provide an answer?

In discussing the second choice Hunter tries his hand at analysis, noting two meanings of culture: (1) "cultus, which any group must transmit"; and (2) "the dominant way of the world in which the cult exists and which exerts influence on the cult and is influenced, in turn, by it."[20] The question immediately obvious is, How is the first part of (2) different from (1)? and further, Is the second part of (2) any more than culture change? Hunter does acknowledge the necessity of the Christian religion to transmit its heritage to the young, but he makes a much stronger point for the task of Christianity as "overcoming the world in which it lives and of which it is a part . . . of changing culture." Indeed, he calls the Christian "some kind of a change agent . . . [in] an essentially godless culture" and prescribes that Christian education must enable the child to become a "change agent for Christ."[21] Hunter is quite correct in his criticism of culture transmission as the only goal for education. There is no reason why value judgments should be limited to cultural norms. We must challenge rigid and obsolete values. But to hold to both transmission and change involves Hunter in a logical contradiction. What he must hold logically is that he favors change which eventually even changes the heritage. Fortunately, Hunter's new title for Christians as "change agents" has been largely ignored.

Hunter's first problem choice reflects the total methodological concern of many theorists. Hunter scores the traditionalist and common Christian education emphasis on "teaching children the faith [e.g., the catechism] . . . as a storehouse of values and knowledge for use" at a later date. He admits that this has some effect, but only as a by-product, and refers to Horace Bushnell to point out the need for a parish-wide program of Christian education related specifically to the present condition (the developmental needs) of every learner. Hunter says, "The parish church . . . is a source of nurture for persons' souls . . . [and] since the Christian religion is fundamentally a means of encountering God now, at every age-level, in every moment of our existence [even God might tire of this!], . . . *engagement* is both the work area and the goal."[22] One can hardly fault Hunter for making a strong case for attention to the reasonable notion of teaching the Christian faith in terms of the child's readiness to learn, but just how precise are the measuring devices used by the research teams in terms of the data involving "the Christian faith"? When one teaches the Christian faith, is one teaching a subject? Obviously, the answers to these questions cannot be given support by the scientific method. Therefore, Hunter turned to a familiar authority pattern and supported the curriculum not on the psychological model he claimed but on the restricted model of prescription. Hunter's description of what a parish educational program *ought to be* ends with an inexplicable notion, his slogan, "engagement is both the work area and the goal."

Hunter's reference to special Christian education methodology prompts a brief look at the methodological concerns of general education. The general question of what to teach, we have seen, is decided on the appeal to value judgments, a philosophical problem. The question of how to teach is also seen to be a philosophical concern beginning with an epistemological answer to What can we know? and How can it be known?, on which debate raged from Plato to Dewey, and still rages; and ending with the secondary question of specific methods of teaching in which the traditional vs. the modern debate also continues. It may be noted that during the second quarter of the twentieth century, the concern for "life problems" has led to an increasing interest in the *how,* or the methodology of teaching. Those who hold that a curriculum must satisfy the needs of the individual as well as the needs of the society are bound to turn to a more flexible organization and program for education. The same could be said of those who emphasize experience or any other slogan or slogan system.

We have argued earlier that any use of "needs" and "experience" as slogans and the curricula founded on them, e.g., the "needs curriculum" and "experience-centered curriculum," are slogan systems developed in order to relate the prescriptions of certain predetermined theological commitments to changes in educational practice. Further, a survey of the foundations literature in Christian education reveals both an attempt to preserve a hearty concern for subject matter and an overwhelming decision to organize the resulting curriculum by way of "how to present the material," rather than fulfilling an announced intention to present a curriculum geared to the question How do children learn? Contemporary theorists are still asking the same question regarding learning as they confront a curriculum and a methodology reflecting the unsettled state of affairs in secular education in these areas.

Claims for furnishing a "center" or a "curriculum organizing principle" in addition to "needs" and "experience" are as diverse as the definitions of curricula itself. The few examples given below will verify this special confusion.

1. Methods for Christian teaching should be life-centered . . . [where] participation is a central factor. . . . The learner . . . participates with Paul, . . . identifies with those who knew the Lord in the flesh . . . made present to the believer . . . by remembrance [and] participation in the historic event. (Cully)[23]
2. Our purpose is always to place God at the center of the educational process. (Miller)[24]
3. If one must speak of a center for curriculum, then it is truest to say that Christ is the center—Christ as we know him only through the Scriptures. . . . But Christ . . . takes the child into the center with him. (*Basic Principles*)[25]
4. A program of Christian teaching must be Church-centered in the sense that it must be fundamentally the Church at work in the nurture of children, youth, and adults. . . . [Its] beginning point [is] the theological thinking of the Church, not general education. (Grimes)[26]
5. This curriculum must center in the I-THOU relationship. In this relationship the crises of life force us to make decisions. . . . Knowledge about religion is not the issue facing us sinners . . . [but] human redemption through the dynamics of the parish [to] develop educational resources that are related to living issues. (Ward)[27]
6. The question [for Christian education] is . . . When *any* method is proposed or used, how do we decide whether or

not it is appropriate? . . . [First,] does it facilitate two-way communication . . . ? [And second,] what is the nature of the interaction which it sets up? . . . *The center of concern in all material and in all methods continues to be communication,* . . . put to a test in experimental use. (Sherrill)[28]

On analysis, Cully's "life-centered" is seen to depend, as she readily admits, "on a deeper connotation through the insights of the existentialist theologians and philosophers."[29] Miller, *Basic Principles,* and Grimes offer homiletical notions to support their "center" for curricula. And *Basic Principles* is using ceremonial language (often a charitable term for nonsense) as it suggests that Jesus Christ "takes the child into the center with him." Since we have thoroughly examined the notion of relationship earlier, it is sufficient here to note that Ward's appeal for educational method and resources is little more than a prescription for certain attitudes and actions congenial to a specific theological point of view. Sherrill also falls victim to the same enthusiasm. With Cully and Ward he presumes an "existential" encounter which is experiential and "bi-polar" but which can be substantiated only on the grounds of prior theological decision and not on the experimental basis he claims. It is regrettable that Sherrill fails to indicate the nature or the results of the "experimental use." As it stands the term is used here only as an "authority figure."

On the application of methodology to educational programs in the churches, several types of methodology are obvious. They are listed here in the order of the adjective used or which seems to describe the method.

1. "do-it-yourself"—The individual himself has the ultimate responsibility for curriculum-building. . . . The task of the curriculum planner in Christian education is not to plan all of educational experience but to [help] the person to focus . . . his experience meaningfully in the gospel. (Wyckoff)[30]
2. "encounter"—Method . . . must always be seen in relation to the ends in view: leading to encounter with the living God and an explication of the meaning of that encounter. (Grimes)[31]

3. "engagement"—A direct outgrowth of our theological imperative. . . . When religious issues are selected as the organizing principle . . . a search begins for the particular manifestations of a given religious issue . . . common at a given age or experience level. . . . If immediate response to God's action is the central objective, . . . the life of the class as observed by the teacher is decisive. (Hunter)[32]

4. "existentialist"—Words alone cannot carry the meaning of the personal response to the gospel. Curriculum needs construction at this point. Christian education needs to develop existential methods, . . . historical remembrance, . . . creative activities, . . . [and] dynamic methods . . . [as] means . . . to empower [growing children] in their every relationship. (Cully)[33]

5. "local-option"—Educational ministry is developed locally. . . . Its goals and . . . plans [and methods] must be designed by those who are on the scene. . . . The fact that each congregation and community are different, and . . . changing . . . means that local churches can no longer depend wholly on national patterns. (Workbook)[34]

6. "progressive"—The Seabury Series goes the whole way toward an acceptance of the educational techniques generally called "progressive." . . . There is no schedule of subjects to cover Sunday by Sunday. Rather, discussion is expected to range freely, with the Bible, the Prayer Book, the Hymnal, the Church Year [etc.] presented as resources for meeting the personal situations [later called "religious issues"] of the children. . . . The object is to guide the children in a relaxed but completely serious discussion of their place in a universe where God, Christ, and the Church are great and meaningful facts . . . [and] to foster a certain religion within the child, namely, the Christian religion . . . [and] to produce not theologians, but Christians. In order to be a Christian, it is necessary to know quite a bit of theology. This is the discovery made by the pupils themselves as they go along. (Peter Day)[35]

7. "redemptive"—Method must serve a redemptive purpose . . . in keeping with the spiritual purpose of Christian education. (Vieth)[36]

8. "situational"—The materials of Christian teaching . . . must be adopted and interpreted so that they are related to

the individual pupil using them in a particular situation. [Method is] a means of bringing the person into a situation where God's revelation may become personally meaningful to him. (*Foundations*)[37]

9. "theological"—The architecture of the curriculum corresponds to these dominant points of theology—Jesus Christ, the Bible, the Church . . . equally Scriptural, theological, and practical. (*Theology in the New Curriculum*)[38]

10. "theology"—Theory for Christian education builds on the evidences from various sources, but it [theology] exercises the right of prior jurisdiction for the reorganization of the material. (Boehlke)[39]

It is scarcely possible to take Wyckoff seriously in his recommendation for individual responsibility, but he seems to so intend. Grimes, Hunter, and Cully all share a belief in the dictation of educational methodology by theological decision. At best, the arguments presented are circular and analytical, true only by definition—"engagement methodology" = "religious issues," which is the consequent of "engagement." And all three offer notions that are so highly prescriptive, e.g., "historical remembrance," that they cannot be considered as foundations for educational method.

"Local option" in any methodological form is bound to be educationally suspect except in the sense in which the parish makes the ultimate decisions and adjustments. Hunter sustains Day's critique of the Seabury Series: "In the early experimental prepublication days of the official curriculum of the Episcopal Church, . . . the curriculum builders were led to the firm decision that the use of religious issues as the organizing principle completely ruled out the possibility of providing teachers with prefabricated lesson plans for each of the Sundays of the year. . . . The official materials for the Episcopal Church continue to emphasize the necessity of tailor-made plans by the teaching team on a week-to-week basis."[40] However, Day's description of the way "religious issues" are to be applied in a learning situation is highly imaginative and prescriptive. An interesting question would be, If it is necessary to know quite a bit of theology to be a Christian, how could anyone be certain that the "local option" of either leader or pupil would elect to "discover" enough theology?

Vieth's reference to "redemptive" method is vacuous, awaiting a theological premise as yet unstated. "Situational" methodology is mostly homiletical and cannot be taken to have serious educational import. Of course, the appeal to theology is obviously proper in discussing the content and method of Christian education. However, such an appeal must be admittedly a justification of educational method that falls short of any empirical or logical verification. While it is quite possible that the words usually associated with educational purpose, content, and method are all available, they can hardly sustain a curriculum in the technical sense of the term.

The main critique of this chapter is thus seen to be that the Christian education theorists and curriculum architects failed to produce a fundation for curricula and methodology which could be identified and justified not simply by the word or prescription of authority, but also by evidence or logic. Indeed, the foundations on which the Christian education curricula and methodology are built not only lack clear definition, but they also are burdened with prescriptive contradictions. Apparently there were as many educational experts as there were ecclesiastical authorities. The inbred nature of the theorists of Christian education committed as they are to the decisions of existentialism, need, experience, fellowship theology, redemptive group life, and so on, could hardly be expected to produce curricula and methodology broader than the limitations of each person's dedication to a certain type of theological and psychological truth.

Another significant item worthy of criticism is the patent and widespread methodological prescriptivity. The truth is that curricula in Christian education is a unique, absolute "thing in itself" and defies comparison with the criteria for curricula in general education. The definitions generally are too broad, e.g., "All that the church and family do," "dynamics of the parish," etc. Further, the stated goal, objective, or purpose of curricula is always theological not educational, and assigned by prescription, e.g., "relationship objectives." While prescriptions are always present in all educational decisions and are of primary significance, general education usually insists upon empirical research and studies as the foundation of a curriculum wherever possible.

Of course, the rejection of "educational traditionalism" by Christian education theorists is quite understandable. No modern educator can ignore the important contributions of scientific psychology; still, the uncritical appeal to research and its use by Christian educators also is highly questionable. We have exposed the slogans and slogan systems built on needs and experience as not based on lists from science, but based on lists prescribed by ecclesiastical fiat. The same is true of the methodological decision of a curriculum organizing principle. We have no argument with the rejection of the traditional subject-matter methodology. What we do score is the notion that engagement or situational methodology is any more scientific. Since neither lists of needs, experiences, nor religious issues are available from science, the methodological prescriptivity is quite obvious.

It is also obvious that the major mechanical problem in Christian education curricula and methodology is the training of teachers who are skilled at recognizing and categorizing need and at encouraging a maximum of experiences in learning, and creative enough to "custom-make" the curriculum and guide the student in a "local-option" method. If Paul Calvin Payne's observation on the actual parochial curricular and methodological status quoted by Kennedy is correct, it is obvious that only chaos will result from following the prescriptions of modern theorists. Payne observed, "What is wanted is a curriculum [that] can be successfully taught by untrained teachers (many of whom are unwilling to take time to prepare their lessons) to students who do not study, meet in brief sessions once a week, and are absent fifty percent of the time."[41] Unless a major change is made in the present institutional programs of education in the churches, it is apparent that a "custom-made" curriculum and "local-option" methodology are neither especially helpful theoretically nor practicable educationally.

CHAPTER XII

Conclusion

AN OVERALL survey of the specific conclusions reached in the preceding chapters reveals both general and particular criticisms. The first general criticism is similar to one of the most common criticisms made by Christian education theorists of the traditional program of education and the philosophies on which these programs were said to be based. Actually, in place of the traditional and authoritarian systems that the theorists condemned, many Christian educators produced "new" grand systems based on the authority of only superficially related "scientific" studies. Several theorists refer to the results of secular experimentation for the justification, for instance, of experience over content emphasis; yet their failure to indicate the nature of, or the results from, the experimentation reduces the authority to an "authority figure."

Another general criticism involves some internal contradictions. While most theorists generally urge an emphasis on age group needs over content, yet some curriculum materials are masterpieces of content and some well beyond the reading and comprehension abilities of the children in the age group to be served. Further, Christian educators seem to promise that "final answers" will be shunned, yet some materials contain "final answers" in the form of dogmatic theological speculations. The teacher, in some instances, is referred to authoritative source books to find the "correct" answers. Modern theorists also recommend that parish leaders develop an educational philosophy and program of their own, and yet the writers present well-tailored theoretical systems complete with slogans and prescriptions.

The final general criticism concerns the unannounced shift from descriptive/explanatory language to prescriptive/evaluative pronouncements and recommendations for educational policy. For instance, it is claimed by many modern theorists that the decision to construct a "needs curriculum" from "needs" is made on the basis of scientific experimentation. However, it is obvious on analysis that while many Christian educators accept the descriptive account of the psychologist, some turn it into prescriptive utterance, "Teach X to meet the needs." Further, the pronouncement that content-centered teaching is not nearly so effective as teaching that begins with the consideration of a person's needs and experiences is widely circulated, and other published materials are condemned because they emphasized content rather than learning through experience. However, on careful scrutiny, no descriptive or empirical language is obvious, only prescriptive or recommending language favoring a specific educational program established on prior value judgments.

The contention of this critique is not with the obvious values passed on to the churches and thus to the Christian community by way of the printed educational materials. Further, only commendation can attend the less controversial decisions of several churches to encourage family worship in the church, to develop a parents' class in the church school, and to take advantage of the renewed interest in the Bible, modern Biblical scholarship, and the methods introduced by lay Bible study.

Rather, the concern here is with the foundations materials, the philosophical decisions evidenced in the writings of many of the major Christian educators whose concepts and theories have been examined in these pages, but also many others who made lesser and supportive contributions. Actually, it is often the committee-type foundations background that is mostly responsible for the category-shifting and the fundamental ambiguities obvious in many of the foundations books, pamphlets, and tracts of Christian education.

In the arena of particular criticism, Part One is an examination of the basic elements of the so-called foundations of education offered under the aegis of the Christian churches. Such elements include: the use or misuse of philosophy in the determination of educational decisions; the purpose of definitions and aims statements in Christian education; and the importance of frank and full discussion of the epistemological issues. Parts Two and Three present a conceptual analysis of the substantive and methodological decisions and commitments made by modern theorists as a basis for educational theory and curricula. The decisions analyzed in the chapters of Part Two and Part Three are: (1) "needs" and the "needs policy" (said to be scientifically established); (2) "experience" or "religious issues" (also considered to be scientific in nature); (3) "relationship theology" (with emphasis on existentialism); (4) the "redemptive fellowship" (with emphasis on group process); (5) novel "teaching" (described as either divine or experiential); (6) special "learning" (said to be a "new theory of learning"); and (7) unique curricula and methodology (both dictated by theological prescription). A summary conclusion of each chapter will follow.

The concluding arguments of the chapters of Part One cluster about one central theme, which is: philosophy correctly defined and used is essential to the future development of the foundations and functions of Christian education. First, Christian educators must accept philosophy as a tool for the analysis of the many vague and ambiguous terms in order to achieve the most perfect clarity and explication possible. Such acceptance will carry with it a thorough examination of the recommending elements of education, namely, epistemology, metaphysics, and ethics, as well as of the theological bases of this special education. It is obvious that very little concept analysis has been directed toward the language of Christian education. Theorists and critics alike will assist in the determination of whether or not Christian education has a future by a frank and open scrutiny of every facet of the discipline. And let it start now with an honest self-evaluation based in part on the unsparing criticism of this work.

Second, it seems necessary to remind Christian educators of the dominating purposes of definitions of Christian education and statements of the aims for education in the churches. On analysis, both the definitions and the aims statements are found to put forward little more than the personal opinions, religious points of view, and the slogan systems of the theorists. Further, while all sorts of definitions and statements of aims are available, in the end they all tend toward a pattern of indoctrination rather than, as many theorists claim, toward the methods of science or, at best, open inquiry into the identification and interpretation of reality. Christian education *is* indoctrination and *does* aim at establishing certain basic beliefs as a foundation for the universally desired free and open discussion.

Third, an immediate and wide-ranging investigation of the relations between epistemology and Christian education must be undertaken. Theorists can no longer avoid the necessity of exposing their decisions on "knowing" to public examination and their statements of appraisal and faith to the same verification processes of philosophical analysis now applied to statements of fact and logic. It is quite obvious that the merger of faith and fact or of concept and perception proposed by some theologians has failed to arouse much general philosophical interest and acceptance. Only frank and honest answers given to the informed modern layman will match his serious inquiry into the status of his beliefs and the support from the grounds of knowledge of those beliefs, whether factual verification or personal or social rationality.

A summary of the concluding arguments of Part Two reveals that many theorists either shift language categories from descriptive to prescriptive or use straight prescription. A good example of this was seen in the decision to meet needs. While certain needs are empirically grounded, the needs statements offered by Christian education theorists contain needs identified not by science but by normative decisions made with reference to predetermined goals. The ultimate decision is reached as a recommendation for an educational program to meet needs. Thus, in spite of the presence in the curriculum-building process of the consulting psychologist, the decision to meet needs is prescriptive and not descriptive.

The decision to emphasize experience involves another example of the shifting of language categories from descriptive to prescriptive, evaluative or metaphysical. "Experience" is used in some instances to refer to empirical observation, but is used mostly either as: (1) a title for a "new" corrective of traditional methodologies; (2) a motivational slogan to create or maintain interest; or (3) a mystical, psychological, or vicarious event usually referred to as religious experience. On further analysis, the general use of "experience" in Christian education is revealed to be either analytical, meaning at the most "Create interest in teaching," or prescriptive, recommending the redundant slogan "We learn through experience."

The commitment to relationship theology implicated Christian educators in both specific ambiguities and serious language shifts. The shift from the ordinary notion of relationship as a connection between living persons to the theological notion where one "person" is God may be supportable by analogy and Biblical language, but seems unsupported as matter-of-fact language on inquiry.

It is also obvious that many of the theorists are not concerned with describing existing relations, but in prescribing what relations should exist, a normative issue. Further, the categories of Buber were shown to be both limited in terms of the wide gamut of human relations, and prescriptive as well. Finally, where there is some justification for an interest on the part of Christian educators in the notion of relationship, its uncritical use as a recommendation for educational policy is questionable.

The commitment to redemptive fellowship also is seen on analysis to contain both a switching of language categories and a value judgment on which an educational program has been built. The most frequent use of "redemptive" by the Christian education theorists is adjectival/prescriptive, prescribing what groups ought to be rather than describing group process as it is. The uncritical use of "redemptive" is one illustration of the correlative commitment to the more popular definition of group dynamics as "techniques and ideology," in contrast to the academic definition as achieving knowledge about groups. Further, both the individual-group paradox latent in the philosophical foundations of Christian education and the persistent dualism noted earlier contributed to several practical educational dilemmas, for instance, Is the group method the best way to learn?

To sum up the concluding arguments of Part Three, Christian educators are observed to arrive at all methodological decisions by outright prescriptions based on prior theological commitments. "Christian teaching" is a good example of this criticism. The notions of "God as teacher" and "teaching through the language of relationship" are both based on theological not educational positions, and cannot otherwise be given meaning or implementation. For instance, if God is acknowledged to be the teacher, what does the human teacher do? Further, the attempt of the theorists to introduce the experiential notion into an explanation of teaching fails, as we have already noted in the discussion of experience, because they are guilty of a shift from descriptive (scientific) to prescriptive language. And the move from "teach" to "train" also fails because the former concept entails much more than the more limited notion of training. Finally, the confusing number of titles given to teachers by almost all of the theorists is a clue to the confusion of concepts of teaching in Christian education. Therefore, the answer to the question posed earlier as to the theoretical and practical meaningfulness of Christian teaching must be negative. Indeed, only as teachers in a church situation function as teachers in the ordinary sense of the term will any teaching occur at all.

"Christian learning" is also a good example of sterile dependency on theological presuppositions as the basis for purpose and objective in learning. As a restatement of Augustinian-Thomistic educational doctrine, the "new theory of learning" must, in the end, rest on the inaccessible foundation of prior theological judgments and concepts. Actually, the Christian theory of learning is a theory in the *sui generis* sense only, and all attempts to give it descriptive validity by reference either to "learning by experience," or "religious issues at all ages" are unmasked as prescriptive based on the theological positions espoused and not on verifiable descriptive bases as claimed. Our analysis has noted the folly of the castigation of all the learning theories from general education since no special category of religious learning can be identified. As in the case of all prescriptive notions, a unique theory of learning lacking valid research studies and the supporting elements of a clear concept of teaching along with curricula and methodology structured in strict accordance with educational criteria and procedures, will be little more than propagational and prescriptive activity.

Special commitments in the area of curricula and methodology by Christian educators also can be faulted for their highly prescriptive foundations. Indeed, special curricula and methodology dictated by theological and not educational purposes and objectives are hardly theoretical foundation enough to sustain a full educational program. The rejection by modern theorists of traditionalism in favor of empirically established educational foundations is a creditable move, yet, as we have noted elsewhere, the move to slogans such as "needs" and "experience" supported by questionable "research" as authority is hardly a gain. This is true of methodology as well as curricula. "Situational" or "engagement" methodology dependent on highly prescriptive "needs," "experience," and "religious issues" is no more "scientific" than any of the more traditional methodological doctrines and practices criticized by the theorists. Finally, such special curricula and methodology are in their theoretical form interesting, but they are technically inapplicable and impractical. Educational programs for a large, universal, and catholic ecclesiastical institution can hardly be based on "custom-made" curricula and/or "local-option" methodology, except as these slogans apply to parochial freedom in planning, revision, and execution of programs.

One final criticism of the position of many of the major theorists must be offered. Since it is the intention of Christian educators to convince people on rational grounds to accept their recommended educational policies (for instance, engagement methodology), it is necessary to ask, What canon of conviction is involved? Of course there is only one answer: policy proposals for Christian education, like those of secular education, ought to stand the test of conceptual analysis and ought not to make pseudoscientific claims that cannot be validated. The use of theological language is obviously necessary and will be acceptable as long as the statements prescribing policies in Christian education are presented for the scrutiny of analysis within the canons of logic. However, in the long run, policy decisions in education cannot depend on prior theological commitments. For instance, it is one thing to state that God provides the faith condition necessary to all knowledge, but such a statement is not a straightforward factual educational foundation. Rather, it is either a call to devotional activity or an attempt to explain an otherwise paradoxical and mystical concept or notion.

It is apparent that churches will continue to organize their personnel and resources to teach something. Therefore, it is imperative that Christian educators continue to put forward answers to the questions of what and how. Further, the discourse must not be in an exclusive, private language, nor carried on in an intramural dialogue between the theorists, but in a forum open for full church discussion and where the judgments made should stand analytical examination. Finally, objectives must be set which are less pretentious than, for instance, making the church a redemptive community. It is enough to set unabashed prescriptions without a mask or front of descriptivity, but equipped with fully examined and precise substantive and methodological concepts and recommendations. Christian education has a built-in advantage worth exploiting. Since the major concern is not so much with learning theory (which is descriptive) as with instructional theory (which is prescriptive), church education can afford to be bold. However, only by a continual process of conceptual analysis of its theories and empirical testing of its programs can Christian education achieve full status as an academic discipline and improve its helpfulness in the life of the churches.

Notes

Chapter I. INTRODUCTION

1. Ralph D. Heim, "The Use of the Bible in Religious Education," in Marvin J. Taylor, ed., *Religious Education*, pp. 62–63.

2. B. Othanel Smith and Robert H. Ennis, eds., *Language and Concepts in Education*, Preface.

3. H. Shelton Smith, *Faith and Nurture*, p. ix.

4. *Theology in the New Curriculum*, p. 2.

Chapter II. PHILOSOPHY AND CHRISTIAN EDUCATION

1. W. N. Pittenger, "The Presuppositions of Religious Education," *The Living Church*, Oct. 3, 1948.

2. W. B. Kennedy, "The Genesis and Development of the *Christian Faith and Life* Series," pp. 557–558.

3. *Ibid.*, p. 557.

4. D. J. O'Connor, *An Introduction to the Philosophy of Education*, p. 3.

5. *Ibid.*, p. 27.

6. Elmer Sprague, *What Is Philosophy?* p. 5.

7. O'Connor, *op. cit.*, p. 45.

8. Alfred North Whitehead, *Adventures of Ideas*, p. 17.

9. Bertrand Russell, "Dewey's New Logic," in Paul A. Schlipp, ed., *The Philosophy of John Dewey*, p. 138.

10. James E. McClellan and B. Paul Komisar, in C. D. Hardie, *Truth and Fallacy in Educational Theory*, p. vi.

11. *Ibid.*, p. viii.

12. *Ibid.*, p. xiii.

13. *Ibid., p.* xv.

14. O'Connor, *op. cit.*, p. 1.

15. *Ibid.,* p. 5.

16. *Ibid.,* p. 14.

17. Kingsley Price, *Education and Philosophical Thought,* p. 9.

18. O'Connor, *op. cit.,* p. 138.

19. *Ibid.,* p. 109.

20. Pittenger, *loc. cit.*

21. V. O. Ward, in Dorothy L. Braun, "A Historical Study of the Origin and Development of the Seabury Series," p. 186; Kennedy, *op. cit.,* p. 67; *Foundations of Christian Teaching in Methodist Churches,* p. 5.

22. Braun, *op. cit.,* p. 283.

23. Basil A. Yeaxlee, *Religion and the Growing Mind,* p. 170; Lewis Joseph Sherrill, *The Gift of Power,* p. xii; Earl F. Zeigler, *Christian Education of Adults,* p. 91.

24. D. Campbell Wyckoff, *The Gospel and Christian Education,* p. 16; Iris V. Cully, *The Dynamics of Christian Education,* p. 78.

25. Albert E. Bailey, "Philosophies of Education and Religious Education," in Taylor, *op. cit.,* p. 30.

26. Frank E. Gaebelein, *Towards a Christian Philosophy of Education,* p. 3.

27. Randolph C. Miller, *The Clue to Christian Education,* p. 2.

28. Sherrill, *The Gift of Power,* pp. 68, 175; Howard Grimes, *The Church Redemptive,* pp. 89, 148; Paul H. Vieth, ed., *The Church and Christian Education,* p. 298; Robert R. Boehlke, *Theories of Learning in Christian Education,* p. 93; Cully, *op. cit.,* pp. 16–17; James D. Smart, *The Teaching Ministry of the Church,* pp. 199, 206.

29. David R. Hunter, interview with the author, Jan. 21, 1965.

30. David R. Hunter, *Christian Education as Engagement,* pp. 30, 31, 28, 31.

31. Nels F. S. Ferré, *A Theology for Christian Education,* pp. 91, 89.

32. Miller, *The Clue to Christian Education,* pp. 5–6.

33. Smart, *op. cit.,* pp. 66–67.

34. Wyckoff, *The Gospel and Christian Education*, p. 79.

CHAPTER III. WHAT IS CHRISTIAN EDUCATION?

1. "What Is Christian Education?" *International Journal of Religious Education*, Vol. 36, No. 1 (Sept., 1959), p. 4.

2. *Ibid.*

3. William B. Williamson, *A Handbook for Episcopalians*, p. 118.

4. Grimes, *op. cit.*, p. 104.

5. Zeigler, *op. cit.*, p. 46.

6. *The International Curriculum Guide: Book One—Principles and Objectives of Christian Education*, p. 9.

7. John Wilson, "Education and Indoctrination," in T. H. B. Hollins, ed., *Aims in Education*, p. 24.

8. Alva I. Cox, Jr., "What Do We Teach?" *International Journal of Religious Education*, Vol. 36, No. 1 (Sept., 1959), p. 14.

9. Sherrill, *The Gift of Power*, pp. 82, 168.

10. Reuel L. Howe, *Man's Need and God's Action*, pp. 52, 114.

11. Fred Paddock, "Christian Education: A Statement," *Drew Gateway*, Vol. 29, No. 1 (Autumn, 1958), p. 99.

12. Randolph C. Miller, *Biblical Theology and Christian Education*, pp. 4, 33.

13. D. Campbell Wyckoff, *The Task of Christian Education*, p. 29.

14. Donald Crawford, *A Parish Workshop in Christian Education*, p. 48.

15. R. E. Rummer, "Christian Education Is Spiritual Nurture," *Religious Education*, Vol. LXI, No. 6 (Nov.–Dec., 1966), p. 447.

16. *Workbook: Developing Your Educational Ministry*, pp. 14, 29.

17. *The Objectives of Christian Education*, p. 4.

18. *The International Curriculum Guide: Book One.*

19. *The Objectives of Christian Education*, pp. 12–13.

20. *Foundations of Christian Teaching in Methodist Churches*, p. 31.

21. *Christian Education in Our Church,* pp. 5, 9.

22. *A Guide for Selecting Curriculum Materials,* p. 5.

23. Wyckoff, *The Task of Christian Education,* p. 118.

24. Dora P. Chaplin, *Children and Religion,* pp. 211, 222; *The Privilege of Teaching,* p. 136.

25. Sherrill, *The Gift of Power,* p. 83.

26. Ferré, *op. cit.,* pp. 183–184.

27. David J. Ernsberger, *A Philosophy of Adult Christian Education,* p. 103.

28. Richard S. Peters, *Authority, Responsibility and Education,* pp. 86, 87.

29. Lewis Joseph Sherrill, *Lift Up Your Eyes,* p. 127.

30. John Dryden, *The Hind and the Panther,* Pt. iii, l. 389.

31. Smart, *op. cit.,* p. 176.

32. Sherrill, *The Gift of Power,* p. 98.

33. Wilson, *op. cit.,* p. 28.

34. *The Parent-Parish Program of Christian Education,* p. 5.

35. W. R. Niblett, quoted by Stanley J. Curtis, *Introduction to the Philosophy of Education,* p. 53.

36. Aristotle, *Nicomachean Ethics,* II.i.

CHAPTER IV. EPISTEMOLOGY AND CHRISTIAN EDUCATION

1. Sprague, *op. cit.,* p. 13.

2. *Ibid.,* p. 13.

3. *Ibid.,* p. 63.

4. *Ibid.,* p. 29.

5. Israel Scheffler, *Conditions of Knowledge: An Introduction to Epistemology and Education,* pp. 13, 74.

6. Sprague, *op. cit.,* p. 64.

7. George F. Kneller, *Introduction to the Philosophy of Education,* p. 9.

8. Jerome S. Bruner, quoted by Kneller, *ibid.,* p. 10.

9. Kneller, *op. cit.,* p. 64.

10. *Ibid.,* p. 47.

11. Harry S. Broudy, *Building a Philosophy of Education,* p. 121.

12. Sprague, *op. cit.*, p. 54.

13. Thomas F. Torrance, *The School of Faith*, p. xxvi.

14. Sara Little, *Learning Together in the Christian Fellowship*, pp. 21–22.

15. Paul L. Lehmann, "The Meaning of the Resurrection," *Counsel*, April–June, 1949, p. 4.

16. D. M. Emmet, in J. V. Langmead Casserley, *The Christian in Philosophy*, p. 187.

17. *Ibid.*, p. 192.

18. O'Connor, *op. cit.*, p. 32.

19. *Ibid.*, p. 34.

20. Smart, *op. cit.*, p. 150.

21. Wyckoff, *The Gospel and Christian Education*, p. 180.

22. D. Campbell Wyckoff, *Theory and Design of Christian Education Curriculum*, p. 20.

23. Mayo Smith, "Education in Relation to the Other Activities of the Church," an unpublished working paper, p. 10.

24. Boehlke, *op. cit.*, pp. 33–34, 169.

25. Ralph R. Sundquist, *Whom God Chooses: The Child in the Church*, pp. 32–33.

26. Cully, *op. cit.*, pp. 34, 77, 87, 99.

27. Miller, *op. cit.*, pp. 16, 71.

28. Charles R. Stinnette, Jr., *Learning in Theological Perspective*, pp. 21, 23, 24, 36.

29. Sherrill, *The Gift of Power*, pp. 72, 90–91, 95.

30. Hunter, *Christian Education as Engagement*, pp. 27, 108–109.

31. Ferré, *op. cit.*, pp. 73, 74, 77.

32. Georgia Harkness, *Foundations of Christian Knowledge*, pp. 81, 109, 117.

33. Ferré, *op. cit.*, p. 31.

CHAPTER V. THE DECISION TO "MEET NEEDS"

1. David R. Hunter, *The New Program of Christian Education*, pp. 1–4.

2. B. Paul Komisar, " 'Need' and the Needs-Curriculum," in Smith and Ennis, *op. cit.*, p. 37.

3. *Ibid.*, p. 39.

4. Sherrill, *Lift Up Your Eyes*, p. 25; *The Gift of Power*, p. 106.

5. S. Little, *op. cit.*, p. 9.

6. Kennedy, *op. cit.*, pp. 122, 146–147.

7. Randolph C. Miller, "Discipline in a Church School Class," *The Witness*, Vol. 42, No. 49 (Dec. 22, 1955), p. 12.

8. Stinnette, *op. cit.*, p. 40.

9. C. G. Miller and R. U. Smith, "Christian Education Milestones at General Convention," *Findings*, Dec., 1958, pp. 8–10.

10. Boehlke, *op. cit.*, p. 122.

11. Howe, *op. cit.*, p. 9.

12. Donald W. Crawford, "Parish, Like Family Life, Is Built on Common Faith," *Churchways*, 1952, p. 10; *A Parish Workshop in Christian Education*, p. 34.

13. Wyckoff, *The Gospel and Christian Education*, p. 158.

14. Lawrence C. Little, "The Objectives of Protestant Religious Education," in Taylor, *op. cit.*, p. 69.

15. *The Functional Objectives for Christian Education*, p. 81.

16. Cully, *op. cit.*, p. 129; "Children's Work in the Church," in Taylor, *op. cit.*, p. 111.

17. Ferré, *op. cit.*, p. 53.

18. Grimes, *op. cit.*, p. 115.

19. *The Objectives of Christian Education*, p. 10.

20. *The International Curriculum Guide: Book One*, p. 69.

21. Yeaxlee, *op. cit.*, p. 54.

22. *The Objectives of Christian Education*, p. 6.

23. *The International Curriculum Guide: Book One*, p. 26.

24. Ferré, *op. cit.*, p. 26.

25. Daniel Day Williams, "Current Theological Developments and Religious Education," in Taylor, *op. cit.*, p. 46.

26. Heim, "The Use of the Bible in Religious Education," in Taylor, *op. cit.*, p. 58.

27. *Basic Principles—Christian Faith and Life*, p. 9.

28. *Church School Teacher's Workshop*, p. 35.

29. Hunter, *Christian Education as Engagement*, p. 36.

30. Edward Farley, "Does Christian Education Need the Holy Spirit?" *Religious Education,* Vol. 60, No. 5 (Sept.–Oct., 1965), p. 345.

Chapter VI. THE DECISION TO EMPHASIZE "EXPERIENCE"

1. John Heuss, "The Story of Our Quest," *Episcopal Churchnews,* Vol. 121 (Oct. 14, 1956), p. 24.

2. William S. Lea, "Some Questions on the Seabury Series," *Episcopal Churchnews,* Vol. 120 (Aug. 7, 1955), p. 16.

3. *Christian Education: Guide I,* p. 8.

4. Paul H. Vieth, in *Bridging Some Gaps,* p. 27.

5. Charles Penniman, in Braun, *op. cit.,* p. 171.

6. Randolph C. Miller, *A Guide for Church School Teachers,* p. 24.

7. Miller, *The Clue to Christian Education,* p. 35.

8. Miller, *A Guide for Church School Teachers,* p. 38.

9. Miller, *The Clue to Christian Education,* p. 2.

10. *Ibid.,* pp. vii–viii.

11. *Ibid.,* p. 4.

12. *Ibid.,* p. 5.

13. *The International Curriculum Guide: Book One,* pp. 18, 23–24, 29, 37, 98.

14. Wyckoff, *The Task of Christian Education,* pp. 32, 34, 36, 111–112.

15. Sherrill, *The Gift of Power,* pp. 91, 110, 137, 69, 140, 143–144.

16. *Ibid.,* p. 189.

17. Howe, *op. cit.,* p. 114.

18. Williams, "Current Theological Developments and Religious Education," in Taylor, *op. cit.,* p. 50.

19. Paul Tillich, *Theology of Culture,* p. 201.

20. Cully, *op. cit.,* pp. 165, 167, 170, 122.

21. David R. Hunter, "The Basis of the 'New Curriculum,'" *The Episcopal Review,* Vol. 6 (June, 1955), p. 15; and *Christian Education as Engagement,* pp. 38, 9.

Chapter VII. THE COMMITMENT TO "RELATIONSHIP THEOLOGY"

1. Quoted by J. V. Langmead Casserley, *Graceful Reason,* p. 83.

2. Martin Buber, *I and Thou,* pp. 8, 4, 11.

3. *Ibid.,* p. 62.

4. Crawford, *op. cit.,* p. 35.

5. *Apostles in the Home,* pp. 29–35.

6. O'Connor, *op. cit.,* p. 116.

7. Chaplin, *The Privilege of Teaching,* pp. 33–34.

8. *Design for Methodist Curriculum,* pp. 13–14.

9. Yeaxlee, *op. cit.,* pp. 159, 171.

10. Ernsberger, *op. cit.,* pp. 63–64.

11. Sherrill, *The Gift of Power,* pp. 44, 45, 13, 157, 54.

12. Miller, *The Clue to Christian Education,* pp. 5–6, 8, 9.

13. *Ibid.,* pp. 8, 9, 13.

14. Miller, *Biblical Theology and Christian Education,* p. 97.

15. Howe, *op. cit.,* pp. 10–11, 40.

16. *Ibid.,* pp. 75, 94–95, 112, 114, 115.

17. Harvey Cox, *The Secular City,* pp. 48–49.

18. S. Little, *op. cit.,* pp. 21, 22.

19. Grimes, *op. cit.,* pp. 26, 50–52.

20. Smart, *op. cit.,* pp. 123, 157, 162.

21. John R. Fry, *A Hard Look at Adult Christian Education,* p. 45.

22. Crawford, *op. cit.,* pp. 18, 44.

23. *Ibid.,* p. 46.

24. Hunter, *Christian Education as Engagement,* pp. 7, 61.

25. Cully, *op. cit.,* pp. 106, 69.

26. Ferré, *op. cit.,* p. 183.

27. Boehlke, *op. cit.,* pp. 163, 106.

28. *Church School Teacher's Workshop,* p. 31.

Chapter VIII. THE COMMITMENT TO "REDEMPTIVE FELLOWSHIP"

1. See Luke 24:21; Acts 20:28; I Cor. 1:30 and 6:19 f.; Gal. 3:13 and 4:4 f.; Eph. 1:7; Col. 1:14 and 4:5; I Tim. 2:5; Titus 2:14; Heb. 9:12; I Peter 1:18; Rev. 5:9.

2. Hunter, *Christian Education as Engagement*, p. 62.

3. Wyckoff, *The Gospel and Christian Education*, pp. 47–48.

4. Casserley, *Graceful Reason*, p. 125.

5. *Ibid.*, p. 127.

6. *Ibid.*, pp. 128–130.

7. *Ibid.*, p. 131.

8. *Ibid.*, p. 133.

9. Crawford, *op. cit.*, pp. 85–86.

10. Cully, *op. cit.*, p. 59.

11. Ernsberger, *op. cit.*, p. 69.

12. Zeigler, *op. cit.*, p. 138.

13. *The Functional Objectives for Christian Education*, p. 94.

14. Reuel L. Howe, "Revolution in Christian Education," *Church Militant*, Vol. LVIII (June, 1955), p. 5.

15. Cully, *op. cit.*, p. 54.

16. Grimes, *op. cit.*, pp. 47–48.

17. Sherrill, *The Gift of Power*, p. xi.

18. Smart, *op. cit.*, p. 87.

19. Hunter, "The Basis of the 'New Curriculum,'" *loc. cit.*, p. 15.

20. Boehlke, *op. cit.*, pp. 166, 121–122.

21. Grimes, *op. cit.*, p. 45.

22. Kennedy, *op. cit.*, p. 117.

23. Miller, *Biblical Theology and Christian Education*, pp. 131, 150.

24. *Design for Methodist Curriculum*, p. 29.

25. Theodore O. Wedel, "Group Dynamics and the Church," *Theology Today*, Vol. X, No. 4 (Jan. 1954), pp. 511–524.

26. James B. Ashbrook, "Theological Dimensions of Renewal Through Small Groups," *Pastoral Psychology*, Vol. 15, No. 145, pp. 23–32.

27. Wedel, *loc. cit.*, p. 513.

28. Ashbrook, *loc. cit.*, p. 24.

29. *Ibid.*, p. 31.

30. See Lowell B. Hazard, "Where two or three . . . ," a special issue, *International Journal of Religious Education*, Vol. XXXIII, No. 9 (May, 1957) p. 3; "Groups at Work," a special issue, *Faith at Work*, Vol. LXXVI (Oct.–Nov., 1963), including especially "When Is a Group Redemptive?" by Ross Snyder; Clyde H. Reid, "Small Groups Are Here to Stay," *Union Seminary Quarterly Review*, Vol. XVIII (May, 1963), pp. 393–403; Kenneth E. Johnson, "Personal Religious Growth Through Small Group Participation," unpublished doctoral dissertation, Pacific School of Religion, May, 1963.

31. C. Ellis Nelson, "Existential Christian Education," *Union Seminary Quarterly Review*, Vol. XIII (May, 1958), pp. 19–27.

32. H. Shelton Smith, *op. cit.*, p. 102.

33. *The International Curriculum Guide: Book One*, p. 42.

34. S. Little, *op. cit.*, pp. 25, 17.

35. G. J. Jud, "Ministry in Colonies and Retreats," in J. L. Casteel, ed., *Spiritual Renewal Through Personal Groups*, p. 88.

36. C. D. Kean, "The Nature of the Tradition in the Christian Faith and Life," *Findings*, April, 1957, p. 7; and "Group Dynamics and the Life of the Church," *Episcopal Churchnews*, Aug., 1957, p. 31.

37. Miller, *Biblical Theology and Christian Education*, p. 141.

38. Grimes, *op. cit.*, pp. 109, 59.

39. Sherrill, *The Gift of Power*, p. 190.

40. Hunter, *Christian Education as Engagement*, pp. 57, 61, 62.

41. Chaplin, *The Privilege of Teaching*, pp. 258–259.

42. Fry, *op. cit.*, pp. 22–23.

43. Dorwin Cartwright and Alvin Zander, eds., *Group Dynamics: Research and Theory*, pp. 5–6.

44. *Ibid.*, p. 9.

45. *Church School Teacher's Workshop*, p. 30.

Chapter IX. ON TEACHING

1. T. W. Manson, *The Teaching of Jesus*, p. 303.

2. Augustine, *Concerning the Teacher*, p. 56.

3. Thomas Aquinas, *Basic Writings of Saint Thomas Aquinas*, ed. by Anton C. Pegis, Vol. II, 9.2, art. 3, and Reply.

4. S. F. Bayne, in Edmund Fuller, ed., *The Christian Idea of Education*, pp. 255–256.

5. *Ibid.*, p. 265.

6. Stinnette, *op. cit.*, p. 80.

7. Wyckoff, *The Gospel and Christian Education*, p. 148.

8. Howard Grimes, "Communication Through Christian Education," *Drew Gateway*, Vol. 29, No. 1 (Autumn, 1958), p. 18.

9. *Foundations of Christian Teaching in Methodist Churches*, p. 42.

10. *Basic Principles—Christian Faith and Life*, p. 10.

11. Ferré, *op. cit.*, p. 139.

12. Iris V. Cully, "Christian Education: Instruction and Nurture," *Religious Education*, Vol. 61, No. 1 (Jan.–Feb., 1966), p. 10.

13. Cully, *op. cit.*, p. 112.

14. Karl Barth, *Church Dogmatics*, IV, 3, 2, p. 871.

15. Ferré, *op. cit.*, p. 171.

16. *The Functional Objectives for Christian Education*, p. 16.

17. Boehlke, *op. cit.*, p. 125.

18. Wyckoff, *Theory and Design of Christian Education Curriculum*, p. 95.

19. Ernsberger, *op. cit.*, p. 42.

20. Smart, *op. cit.*, p. 11.

21. Cully, *op. cit.*, pp. 46, 105–109, 112.

22. Ward, quoted in Braun, *op. cit.*, p. 185.

23. Howe, *op. cit.*, pp. 69–70, 71, 68.

24. *Ibid.*, pp. 115–117.

25. Mary Jane Aschner, "The Language of Teaching," in Smith and Ennis, *op. cit.*, pp. 112–113, 124–125.

26. B. Othanel Smith, "On the Anatomy of Teaching," *The Journal of Teacher Education*, Vol. VII, No. 4 (Dec., 1956).

27. B. Paul Komisar, "Teaching: Act and Enterprise," *Studies in Philosophy and Education,* Vol. VI, No. 2 (Spring, 1968), pp. 168, 173, 180, 181.

28. B. Paul Komisar, "Conceptual Analysis of Teaching," *High School Journal,* Vol. 50 (Oct., 1966), pp. 21, 20.

29. Scheffler, *op. cit.,* pp. 10–11, 107.

30. Hunter, *Christian Education as Engagement,* p. 50.

31. Ralph Harper, "Significance of Existence and Recognition for Education," *N.S.S.E. Yearbook,* 1955, Pt. I, p. 231.

32. Smart, *op. cit.,* pp. 20, 107, 73–74.

33. *Ibid.,* pp. 19, 165.

34. Grimes, *op. cit.,* p. 89, and *loc. cit.,* p. 15; Ross Snyder, "Members One of Another," *International Journal of Religious Education,* Vol. 33, No. 9 (May, 1957), p. 8; *Foundations of Christian Teaching in Methodist Churches,* p. 39; Ralph N. Mould, *How to Score in Sunday School Work,* p. 4; *Workbook: Developing Your Educational Ministry,* p. 60; Miller, *Biblical Theology and Christian Education,* p. 12; Vieth, *op. cit.,* p. 90.

35. Stinnette, *op. cit.,* pp. 48, 75; Smart, *op. cit.,* p. 206; Sherrill, *The Gift of Power,* p. 121; Chaplin, *The Privilege of Teaching,* p. 34; Yeaxlee, *op. cit.,* p. 201; Kennedy, *op. cit.,* p. 232 (quoting Dr. Payne); Hunter, *Christian Education as Engagement, passim;* Howe, *op. cit., passim.*

36. B. O. Smith, *loc. cit.*

CHAPTER X. ON LEARNING

1. B. Othanel Smith, "A Concept of Teaching," in Smith and Ennis, *op. cit.,* pp. 88–90.

2. Smith, "On the Anatomy of Teaching," *The Journal of Teacher Education,* Vol. VII, No. 4 (Dec., 1956).

3. B. Paul Komisar, "Learning," unpublished paper.

4. Peters, *op. cit.,* pp. 119, 129.

5. *Ibid.,* pp. 134, 136.

6. Albert E. Best, "The Suppressed Premise in Educational Psychology," *Universities Quarterly,* Vol. 16, No. 3 (June, 1962), p. 291.

7. Joseph Manusov, "How Is Learning Possible?" unpublished M.A. thesis, Temple University, 1964, p. 26.

8. Thomas Aquinas, *The Teacher—The Mind,* pp. 16–17.

9. Smart, in Kennedy, *op. cit.,* p. 312; *The International Curriculum Guide: Book One,* p. 12; Ferré, *op. cit.,* p. 119; Boehlke, *op. cit.,* p. 21; Robert J. Havighurst, *The Educational Mission of the Church* (The Westminster Press, 1965), p. 46; Stinnette, *op. cit.,* p. 32; *The Age-Group Objectives of Christian Education,* p. 4; *Design for Methodist Curriculum,* p. 23; Sherrill, *The Gift of Power,* p. 174; S. Little, *op. cit.,* p. 15.

10. G. E. Koehler, "Some Methodist Hopes," *Religious Education,* Vol. 61, No. 3 (May, 1966), p. 201; *The International Curriculum Guide: Book One,* p. 18; Zeigler, *op. cit.,* p. 133; Wyckoff, *Theory and Design of Christian Education Curriculum,* p. 144; Paul B. Maves, "The Christian Education of Adults," in Taylor, *op. cit.,* p. 139; Miller, *Biblical Theology and Christian Education,* p. 41; Boehlke, *op. cit.,* pp. 107, 182; Stinnette, *op. cit.,* pp. 85, 68; *The Functional Objectives for Christian Education,* p. 19; Grimes, *op. cit.,* p. 93; Ernsberger, *op. cit.,* p. 118; Cully, *op. cit.,* p. 135.

11. Anon., "How Do We Learn?" *International Journal of Religious Education,* Sept., 1959, p. 7.

12. Sherrill, *The Gift of Power,* pp. 145, 171, 176.

13. Ferré, *op. cit.,* pp. 109–110, 115, 154–155.

14. Stinnette, *op. cit.,* pp. 11, 88, 28, 85, 13.

15. Grimes, *op. cit.,* p. 93; "Communication Through Christian Education," *loc. cit.,* p. 20.

16. S. Little, *op. cit.,* pp. 15, 26.

17. O'Connor, *op. cit.,* pp. 92, 110.

18. Boehlke, *op. cit.,* pp. 10–11, 20, 128, 186, 189, 192, 201.

19. David R. Hunter, "The Church's Teaching," *International Journal of Religious Education,* Jan., 1964, reprinted.

20. Hunter, *Christian Education as Engagement,* pp. 45, 44.

21. *Ibid.,* p. 16.

22. *Ibid.,* pp. 29, 30.

23. *Ibid.,* pp. 47–48.

24. Randolph C. Miller, "The Demand Is Answered," *Episcopal Churchnews,* Vol. 121 (Oct. 14, 1956), p. 38.

25. Hunter, "The Church's Teaching," *loc. cit.*

CHAPTER XI. ON CURRICULA AND METHODOLOGY

1. Philip H. Phenix, *Philosophy of Education*, p. 57.

2. Broudy, *op. cit.*, pp. 283–285.

3. Phenix, *op. cit.*, p. 59.

4. James D. Butler, *Religious Education*, pp. 263–264.

5. Anon., "Curriculum Is Custom-Made," *International Journal of Religious Education*, Sept., 1959, p. 18.

6. *The International Curriculum Guide: Book One*, pp. 18–19.

7. Vieth, *op. cit.*, pp. 134–135.

8. Ernsberger, *op. cit.*, p. 53.

9. Kennedy, *op. cit.*, p. 667.

10. D. Campbell Wyckoff, "The Curriculum and the Church School," in Taylor, *op. cit.*, p. 99.

11. Grimes, *op. cit.*, p. 103.

12. Braun, *op. cit.*, p. 185.

13. *Workbook: Developing Your Educational Ministry*, p. 34.

14. *Foundations of Christian Teaching in Methodist Churches*, p. 44.

15. Dorothy Scott, quoted in Braun, *op. cit.*, p. 168.

16. Hunter, *Christian Education as Engagement*, pp. 11, 12, 17, 20.

17. *Ibid.*, pp. 20–22.

18. *Ibid.*, p. 57.

19. Don Frank Fenn, "A Parish Priest Looks at the Seabury Series," *ACU News*, May, 1955.

20. Hunter, *Christian Education as Engagement*, pp. 17–18.

21. *Ibid.*, pp. 18–20.

22. *Ibid.*, pp. 14–16.

23. Cully, *op. cit.*, pp. 119–121, 129.

24. Miller, *Biblical Theology and Christian Education*, p. 48.

25. *Basic Principles—Christian Faith and Life*, p. 17.

26. Grimes, *op. cit.*, p. 90.

27. Ward quoted in Braun, *op. cit.*, p. 171.

28. Sherrill, *The Gift of Power*, pp. 184–185, 186.

29. Cully, *op. cit.*, p. 119.

30. Wyckoff, *Theory and Design of Christian Education Curriculum,* pp. 204, 171.

31. Grimes, *op. cit.*, p. 147.

32. Hunter, *Christian Education as Engagement,* pp. 31, 38, 41.

33. Cully, *op. cit.*, pp. 173, 174, 175, 177.

34. *Workbook: Developing Your Educational Ministry,* p. 27.

35. Peter Day, "Revolution in the Sunday School," *The Living Church,* Aug. 7, 1955, p. 17.

36. Vieth, *op. cit.*, p. 214.

37. *Foundations of Christian Teaching in Methodist Churches,* pp. 34, 39.

38. *Theology in the New Curriculum,* p. 9.

39. Boehlke, *op. cit.*, p. 18.

40. Hunter, *Christian Education as Engagement,* pp. 43–44.

41. Paul Calvin Payne, in Kennedy, *op. cit.*, p. 177.

General Bibliography

Aquinas, Thomas, *The Teacher—The Mind*, tr. by James V. McGlynn, S.J. Henry Regnery Company, 1959.

Augustine, Aurelius, *Concerning the Teacher and On the Immortality of the Soul*, tr. by George G. Leckie. Appleton-Century-Crofts, Inc., 1938.

Barth, Karl, *Church Dogmatics*. Edinburgh: T. & T. Clark, 1936.

Boehlke, Robert R., *Theories of Learning in Christian Education*. The Westminster Press, 1962.

Braun, Dorothy L., "A Historical Study of the Origin and Development of the Seabury Series." Unpublished doctoral dissertation, New York University, 1960.

Broudy, Harry S., *Building a Philosophy of Education*. Prentice-Hall, Inc., 1954.

Buber, Martin, *I and Thou*, tr. by Ronald Gregor Smith. Edinburgh: T. & T. Clark, 1937.

Butler, James D., *Religious Education*. Harper & Row, Publishers, Inc., 1962.

Cartwright, Dorwin, and Zander, Alvin, (eds.), *Group Dynamics: Research and Theory*. 2d ed. Harper & Row, Publishers, Inc., 1960.

Casserley, J. V. Langmead, *The Christian in Philosophy*. London: Faber & Faber, Ltd., 1951.

———— *Graceful Reason*. The Seabury Press, Inc., 1954.

Casteel, J. L. (ed.), *Spiritual Renewal Through Personal Groups*. Association Press, 1957.

Chaplin, Dora P., *Children and Religion*. Charles Scribner's Sons, 1948.

———— *The Privilege of Teaching*. Morehouse-Barlow Co., 1962.

Cox, Harvey, *The Secular City*. The Macmillan Company, 1965.

Crawford, Donald, *A Parish Workshop in Christian Education*. The Seabury Press, Inc., 1953.

Cully, Iris V., *The Dynamics of Christian Education*. The Westminster Press, 1958.

Curtis, Stanley J., *Introduction to the Philosophy of Education*. London: University Tutorial Press, 1958.

Ernsberger, David J., *A Philosophy of Adult Christian Education*. The Westminster Press, 1959.

Ferré, Nels F. S., *A Theology for Christian Education*. The Westminster Press, 1967.

Fry, John R., *A Hard Look at Adult Christian Education*. The Westminster Press, 1961.

Fuller, Edmund (ed.), *The Christian Idea of Education*. Yale University Press, 1957.

Gaebelein, Frank E., *Towards a Christian Philosophy of Education*. Winona Lake, Indiana: The Bauman Memorial Lectures Grace College and Theological Seminary, 1962.

Grimes, Howard, *The Church Redemptive*. Abingdon Press, 1958.

Hardie, Charles D., *Truth and Fallacy in Educational Theory*. Teachers College Press, Columbia University, 1962.

Harkness, Georgia, *Foundations of Christian Knowledge*. Abingdon Press, 1955.

Hollins, T. H. B. (ed.), *Aims in Education*. Manchester, England: Manchester University Press, 1964.

Howe, Reuel L., *Man's Need and God's Action*. The Seabury Press, Inc., 1953.

Hunter, David R., *Christian Education as Engagement*. The Seabury Press, Inc., 1963.

Kennedy, W. B., "The Genesis and Development of the *Christian Faith and Life* Series." Unpublished Ph.D. dissertation, Vols. I and II, Yale University, 1957.

Kneller, George F., *Introduction to the Philosophy of Education*. John Wiley & Sons, Inc., 1964.

Little, Sara, *Learning Together in the Christian Fellowship*. John Knox Press, 1956.

Manson, T. W., *The Teaching of Jesus.* Cambridge University Press, 1931.

Miller, Randolph C., *Biblical Theology and Christian Education.* Charles Scribner's Sons, 1956.

———— *The Clue to Christian Education.* Charles Scribner's Sons, 1950.

———— *A Guide for Church School Teachers.* Cloister Press, Ltd., 1943.

Mould, Ralph N., *How to Score in Sunday School Work.* Board of Christian Education, Presbyterian Church in the U.S.A., 1951.

O'Connor, D. J., *An Introduction to the Philosophy of Education.* London: Routledge & Kegan Paul, Ltd., 1963.

Pegis, Anton C. (ed.), *Basic Writings of Saint Thomas Aquinas.* Random House, Inc., 1944.

Peters, Richard S., *Authority, Responsibility and Education.* London: George Allen & Unwin, Ltd., 1960.

Phenix, Philip H., *Philosophy of Education.* Henry Holt and Company, Inc., 1958.

Price, Kingsley, *Education and Philosophical Thought.* Allyn and Bacon, Inc., 1962.

Scheffler, Israel, *Conditions of Knowledge: An Introduction to Epistemology and Education.* Scott, Foresman and Company, 1965.

Schilpp, Paul A. (ed.), *The Philosophy of John Dewey.* Northwestern University Press, 1939.

Sherrill, Lewis Joseph, *The Gift of Power.* The Macmillan Company, 1955.

———— *Lift Up Your Eyes.* John Knox Press, 1949.

———— *The Rise of Christian Education.* The Macmillan Company, 1944.

Smart, James D., *The Teaching Ministry of the Church.* The Westminster Press, 1954.

Smith, B. Othanel, and Ennis, Robert H. (eds.), *Language and Concepts in Education.* Rand McNally & Company, 1961.

Smith, H. Shelton, *Faith and Nurture.* Charles Scribner's Sons, 1941.

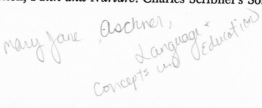

Sprague, Elmer, *What Is Philosophy?* Oxford University Press, Inc., 1961.

Stinnette, Charles R., Jr., *Learning in Theological Perspective.* Association Press, 1965.

Sundquist, Ralph R., *Whom God Chooses: The Child in the Church.* The Geneva Press, 1964.

Taylor, Marvin J. (ed.), *Religious Education: A Comprehensive Survey.* Abingdon Press, 1960.

Tillich, Paul, *Theology of Culture,* ed. by Robert C. Kimball. Oxford University Press, Inc., 1964.

Torrance, Thomas F., *The School of Faith.* London: James Clarke & Co., Ltd., 1959.

Vieth, Paul H. (ed.), *The Church and Christian Education.* The Bethany Press, 1947.

Whitehead, Alfred North, *Adventures of Ideas.* The New American Library, Inc., 1955.

Williamson, William B., *A Handbook for Episcopalians.* Morehouse-Barlow Co., 1961.

Wyckoff, D. Campbell, *The Gospel and Christian Education.* The Westminster Press, 1959.

—— *The Task of Christian Education.* The Westminster Press, 1955.

—— *Theory and Design of Christian Education Curriculum.* The Westminster Press, 1961.

Yeaxlee, Basil A., *Religion and the Growing Mind.* The Seabury Press, Inc., 1952.

Zeigler, Earl F., *Christian Education of Adults.* The Westminster Press, 1958.

PAMPHLETS AND WORKBOOKS

The Age-Group Objectives of Christian Education. Board of Parish Education, The Lutheran Church in America, 1958.

Apostles in the Home. The Seabury Press, Inc., 1956.

Basic Principles—Christian Faith and Life. Board of Christian Education, Presbyterian Church in the U.S.A., 1947.

Bridging Some Gaps. National Council, Protestant Episcopal Church, 1949.

Christian Education: Guide I. National Council, Protestant Episcopal Church, no date.

Christian Education in Our Church. Board of Christian Education, The United Presbyterian Church in the U.S.A., 1959.

The Church Looks Ahead to the New Curriculum—Specifications. National Council, Protestant Episcopal Church, 1950.

Church School Teacher's Workshop. Department of Christian Education, Protestant Episcopal Church, mimeographed, 1954.

The Church's Teaching: An Introduction. by Theodore O. Wedel. National Council, Protestant Episcopal Church, 1949.

Design for Methodist Curriculum General Board of Education, The Methodist Church, 1965.

Foundations of Christian Teaching in Methodist Churches. General Board of Education, The Methodist Church, 1960.

The Functional Objectives for Christian Education. The Boards of Parish Education of The Lutheran Church in America and The American Lutheran Church, 1959.

A Guide for Selecting Curriculum Materials. National Council, Protestant Episcopal Church, 1962.

The International Curriculum Guide: Book One—Principles and Objectives of Christian Education. The International Council of Religious Education, 1932.

The New Program of Christian Education, by David R. Hunter. National Council, Protestant Episcopal Church, 1953.

The Objectives of Christian Education (with study guide). The Boards of Parish Education of The Lutheran Church in America and The American Lutheran Church, 1957.

The Parent-Parish Program of Christian Education. National Council, Protestant Episcopal Church, 1949.

Theology in the New Curriculum. Board of Christian Education, Presbyterian Church in the U.S.A., 1954.

Workbook: Developing Your Educational Ministry. General Board of Education, The Methodist Church, 1967.

Index